PRINCESS

PRINCESS

ROBERT LACEY

Designed by

MICHAEL RAND

Times
BOOKS

Picture research by Vincent Page
Decorated initials designed by The Partnership

Produced for Times Books by
Bellew & Higton Publishers Ltd,
17-21 Conway Street, London W1P 6JD

First published 1982

Text © Robert Lacey 1982

Design and picture selection © Michael Rand 1982

Set in Garamond by V & M Graphics Ltd,
Aylesbury, Bucks.

ALL RIGHTS RESERVED

Times Books
3 Park Avenue, New York, NY 10016

ISBN 0 8129 1017 6

Printed in USA

Contents

To Scarlett
and Selina,
our princesses

LADY DI

Future princess: Lady Diana Spencer, Switzerland, 1978

nce upon a time there was quite an ordinary girl who became a princess. It is a short story, and very simple. She fell in love with a prince and he, warmed by her affection, fell in love with her. When the world found out about it, everyone rejoiced. Loyal subjects in tens of thousands thronged the streets to cheer her on her wedding day. The Archbishop of Canterbury, dressed in shimmering silver, compared this young girl's story to a fairy tale, and no one could seriously quarrel with that comparison. Some people, of course, think that the world should have outgrown princesses. But most of us like fairy tales. . . .

This book celebrates the Princess of Wales. It is not a biography – she is far too young for that. Nor does it attempt to pursue very far the eccentricities of the human psyche that lead us to single out a few of our fellow human beings – like her – to set them apart, and then to bestow upon them affection, loyalty and respect which no rational process of thought can either justify or destroy.

She is not yet the stuff of weighty tomes. She is a joy, good news celebrated by Britain and the wider world. Young, pretty, charming, she has a naturalness that has won over even those customarily unmoved by the royal vaudeville. She is everybody's sweetheart, a national pin-up of the nicest sort. And she is only just twenty-one!

There is a sense, of course, in which we would have welcomed any girl with whom the Prince of Wales fell in love. The blood had to be renewed, the King-to-be had to have a companion, and the nation would have rejoiced gladly in almost any sympathetic young bride.

But this girl evidently has something extra. No sooner was she engaged than etiquette experts started worrying about her name. Diana is not traditional to the British royal family. The suggestion was made that she should properly be known as 'the Princess Charles'. But nobody took any notice, for Her Royal Highness the Princess of Wales is clearly a person in her own right, and to most of the world she remains 'Lady Di'.

Early in September 1980, James Whitaker, most houndlike of all Fleet Street's newshounds, was stalking his favourite prey. Prince Charles was fishing in the River Dee near Balmoral, and the Prince was, apparently, on his own.

But then suddenly Whitaker saw a flash of light. It came from near the base of a pine tree, just a few yards away from where the Prince was standing – and training his binoculars on the tree, Whitaker could see the tip of a green Wellington boot. Somebody was with the Prince, and whoever it was was observing the observers with the help of a hand mirror which had caught the sunlight.

The photographers with Whitaker went into action. Up river one of them trained a 500-mm lens on the left-hand side of the crucial tree trunk. His colleague moved downstream to cover the other side. Whichever way the Prince's companion retreated, the sleuths felt sure they would get a picture.

But they were wrong. As the double flanking exercise went into operation, the quarry sat tight, unwilling to be panicked. Then swiftly and deliberately the lady rose, turned and walked straight up a hill, whose gradient Whitaker reckoned at one in two, without so much as turning her head. She was wearing a headscarf which hid her face from both sides, and a flat cap pulled down low, so that the newsmen got scarcely a glimpse of her features.

The press posse could hazard no guess at the identity of the Prince of Wales's new companion. But whoever she might be, she was clearly going to make a worthy opponent....

The girl who was, within twelve months, to become the most photographed woman in the world had made a spirited debut. Fresh, sparky and stylish, Lady Diana Spencer was about to capture the heart of a nation, and she did it by capturing the heart of a prince.

They had known each other ever since childhood. But when they got engaged, it was quite a recent meeting in a ploughed field that they both remembered.

'It was 1977,' said Lady Diana. 'Prince Charles came to stay as a friend in my father's house for a shoot.'

'I remember thinking,' said Prince Charles, 'what a very jolly and amusing and attractive sixteen-year-old she was. I mean, great fun – bouncy and full of life and everything.'

And what did Lady Diana think of *him*? 'Pretty amazing.'

It was not long before such phrases had inspired a self-contained Lady Di lexicography: 'quite dreadful', 'all this fuss', 'hopefully', 'so daunting', 'absolutely maddening', 'very cross' and 'a great challenge'. Cognoscenti recognized this as the vocabulary of girls with names like Muffy and Fergie, who meet for tea in places like Fortnum's. To the wider world she sounded just how a princess should be.

'Being royal is like getting into a cold bath,' says Prince Charles in the play *Her Royal Highness?*, the wobbly theatrical curtsey which, within months of the wedding, was regaling West End audiences with fanciful details of the royal romance. 'It's very wet and you can never get out of it.'

The stage prince then goes on to teach his fiancée various royal tricks – how to wave for hours so that her arm will not ache, how to make her standard inquiries about the work, homes and hobbies of district nurses and lord mayors sound fresh and natural every time.

But the great thing about the real Lady Di was that she did not need any lessons at being fresh and natural. She seemed made to be a princess – and, in a sense, she was.

Park House, Sandringham

She was born in the early evening of 1 July 1961 at Park House, Sandringham, a few hundred yards from the great house where the royal family have been coming for their holidays since the days of Edward VII. So she was, quite literally, the girl next door, which was one more cause for celebration when the engagement was announced.

Sandringham looks like any other country estate, but somehow it isn't. The gates don't sag, the roads are neatly tarred and cambered, and the hedges look freshly clipped – which they have been. Well-funded estate management has discreetly stage-managed the countryside to put on the best possible showing for its royal owner, and the same goes for the ordinary-looking houses scattered around the neighbourhood. There is nothing on the outside to suggest that their occupants are special in any way, but in fact they are – courtiers of varying degrees, since the distinction between royal companionship and royal service is not always a clear one.

It was as such royal friends and helpers that the future Earl Spencer and his wife Frances were occupying Park House in the early 1960s. He was a former equerry to the Queen. Sharing the royal family's enthusiasm for field sports, he had been with the Queen's father, George VI, on the great day that the King shot his thousandth woodcock.

His wife Frances was the daughter of Ruth, Lady Fermoy, lady-in-waiting to Queen Elizabeth the Queen Mother, and her own birth twenty-five years earlier in Park House had coincided with the death of King George V in the main house nearby. It is said that Queen Mary's first thought on rising from beside her husband's deathbed in January 1936 was to inquire after the health of Ruth Fermoy and of the new Fermoy baby, and those who see monarchy in mystical terms draw breath at the sixth sense by which the old Queen could divine the role that this new-born child, mother to the next Princess of Wales, would one day play in the succession.

The first Lady Diana Spencer lived in the eighteenth century. Her grandmother, the formidable Sarah, Duchess of Marlborough, called her 'Di', and had plans to make her the wife of Frederick, Prince of Wales, son of George II, until the Prime Minister, Robert Walpole, found out what was going on. Still, if at first you don't succeed....

1961 was a good year for spacemen (Yuri Gagarin), black African independence (Sierra Leone and Tanzania), and volcanoes (Tristan da Cunha). It was a bad year for Nazis (Adolf Eichmann), invasions (the Bay of Pigs) and railway trains (the Orient Express made its last journey from Paris to Budapest). A new Austin Mini cost £350, plus £146 19s. 2d. purchase tax; Mrs Margaret Thatcher was parliamentary secretary to the Minister of Pensions and National Insurance; and Prince Charles Philip Arthur George was a twelve-year-old boarder at Cheam Preparatory School in Hampshire.

On her wedding day Lady Diana Spencer distinguished her last unprincessly seconds by muddling up the names of her husband-to-be.

1961: Diana Spencer with her parents at her christening

This convinced the world that she was human, if anyone still needed convincing, and she exhibited from an early age the soft-heartedness which was to endear her so rapidly to so many. She was, recalls her mother, particularly fond 'of anything in a small cage'.

'She loved her soft toys nearly as much as she loved babies,' recalls her father. 'She always loved babies.'

First birthday

Her parents separated when she was six. At the time of her engagement some inquirers burrowed enthusiastically into this. The much publicized custody battle between her father and the Hon. Mrs Shand Kydd, as her mother soon became, offered one stain of scandal on an otherwise shining escutcheon.

Social commentators noted the significance of a divorced couple riding in open carriages through the cheering streets on the wedding day, sitting proudly beside the sovereign and her escort – the Queen accompanying Earl Spencer, Prince Philip escorting Mrs Peter Shand Kydd back to Buckingham Palace. Amateur psychologists wondered whether this early family tragedy had not contributed to the Princess's evident realism, and the resilience with which she had so cheerfully withstood all the pressures attendant on her most extraordinary courtship and marriage.

Her family had a nickname for her – 'Duchess'. She seemed so composed, so very sure of herself. She knew what she wanted, and she was good at getting it – and she needed to be when, at the age of nine, she was sent away to school. Until then she had been educated cosily at home by Gertrude Allen, the governess who had taught her mother before her. Now suddenly she had to accustom herself to the world of playing fields, dormitories, communal changing rooms and compulsory baths. It was hard work for a child whom her family remember as 'home-loving': 'Diana really did not enjoy going away very much.'

Her new school, Riddlesworth Hall, near Thetford in Norfolk, did its best to soften the transition for its little girls. Each was encouraged to bring her own pet to live with her at school, a small hamster or guinea pig she could cuddle and care for, and these furry friends occupied a shantytown of hutches in a grove of yew trees opposite the front door. One holiday, her tan and white guinea pig, Peanuts, won first prize in the Fur and Feather section of the Sandringham Show. At Park House she kept a ginger cat called Marmalade and a grey pony – though, having had a nasty fall at the age of eight, she was not fond of riding.

With Peanuts, the prize-winning guinea pig

Alfred Betts, who was her father's butler in the years after the divorce, remembers a quiet, reserved girl, trying hard to hide the anxiety of going back to school at the end of every holiday by getting her tuck box filled up with chocolate cake, Twiglets and ginger biscuits. He describes her as a 'self-reliant, loving, domesticated' sort of child.

'She washed and ironed her own jeans and did all her own chores.'

She did not shine at school, but she did like English history. Perhaps this was because it was about families that she knew. The Spencers have a pedigree going back to Saxon times. They made their fortune in sheep in the later Middle Ages and they can number in their genealogy forebears such as the first, seventeenth-century, Sir Winston Churchill. They can also claim connection with the blood royal through several mistresses of the brothers Charles II and James II.

The aim at Riddlesworth Hall was to get its young charges 'facing forward', which meant giving them poise and manners, and with the Hon. Diana Spencer (she did not become Lady Diana until her father succeeded to the earldom in 1975), the school succeeded. She was clearly not destined to win a Nobel Prize, but she was kind and cheerful, and she always tried hard. Her former headmistress now remembers particularly the sympathy she showed for younger girls as she rose higher through the school: 'She was awfully sweet with the little ones.'

A couple of Union Jacks are draped from the windows of two semidetached houses in St Mary's Road, Tetbury. It is a snowy day in December 1981 and the Princess of Wales is coming to call.

Soon after the announcement of Prince Charles's engagement to the Lady Diana Spencer in February 1981, the children of St Mary's Church of England Junior School wrote to offer their congratulations and to invite her to come over and visit them.

On 14 August 1981 they received their answer. The Princess would love to come on Tuesday, 8 December, so here she is, driving up St Mary's Road at the wheel of her silver Ford Escort, discreetly tailed by two cube-shaped bodyguards in a large Ford Granada, and several hundred assorted cameramen, journalists and local well-wishers.

Inside the school the children's recorder orchestra is giving a rendering of 'Unto Us a Boy is Born', though, to the disappointment of the journalists, the Princess does not arrive in the hall until after this particular carol has been completed. She listens to 'While Shepherds Watched' and 'O Come All Ye Faithful', then the vicar gives his blessing, as he does every Tuesday, and it is time for the tour to start.

Class 4W are doing what used to be called 'sums', when the twenty-year-old Princess walks into their room – though they explain to her that they are doing 'shapes of five. We've got to put all sorts of fives together.'

'Who ate the yoghurt in all these yoghurt pots?' asks the royal visitor. 'I've never been much of a mathematician.'

The teacher of 4W, Janice Walker, explains to the Princess that this year's class is the smallest she's ever had to teach.

'*That* must be a relief,' says the Princess.

Bridesmaid (second left) at the age of eight

Janice Walker actually went to see the royal wedding. She boarded a bus from Bristol in the middle of the night with a couple of other teachers from St Mary's, arrived in London at five in the morning, and secured a prime position on the steps of the Victoria Memorial.

'That was me spread-eagled up against the railings,' she says.

'Did you watch the wedding on TV?' the Princess asks one little girl. 'Did you like the wedding dress?'

'Do you know all your tables?' she asks another. 'You really should.'

Amanda Grant presents the visitor with a calendar featuring special baby pictures for the coming June and July.

'What sort of baby is it in the basket?' asks the Princess. 'Is it a boy or is it a girl? Perhaps it will be one of each.'

The Princess of Wales spends just twelve minutes with 4W, but afterwards they all have a lot to say about it.

'Her eyes were very blue.'

'I didn't realize she would be so tall.'

'She knelt by every single table.'

'She kept fiddling with her engagement ring.'

'I didn't think she'd drive her own car. I thought she'd come in a Rolls Royce, not an Escort.'

One brave girl had asked if Prince Charles would come to the school one day.

'I'll make him come,' replied the Princess.

Schoolgirl, near her mother's London flat in 1968

Diana Spencer started at a new school when she was twelve – West Heath, a small, middle-ranking academy in Sevenoaks, Kent – and the pin-up picture on her dormitory wall was of Prince Charles, wearing the ceremonial robes of his 1969 investiture at Caernarvon.

The Spencer girls had kept up their friendship with the younger members of the House of Windsor. Park House had a new heated swimming pool, the only pool on the Sandringham estate, and this attracted visits from Prince Andrew and Prince Edward. Spending half her holidays at Sandringham, the future Princess of Wales acquired an unusually close view of royalty off duty. There are not many little girls who grow up with Queen Elizabeth II living at the bottom of the garden.

In her early teens Diana Spencer started spending long periods of her holidays in Scotland, on the Isle of Seil near Oban, where her mother's new husband, Peter Shand Kydd, moved to set up as a beef farmer. Mrs Shand Kydd occupied herself with a toy shop in Oban called Menzies – which misled one reporter into describing her as 'the manageress of a well-known

Holidays in Scotland, with Soufflé, a Shetland pony

Country hat. On holiday in Scotland

Town hat. Long hair and sophistication

stationers' – so when the young Spencers were not at school, they shuttled between their parents, mackerel fishing and lobster potting on the west coast of Scotland, and driving a pale blue beach buggy around the grounds of Althorp (sometimes pronounced Allthrup or even Alltrup), the ancestral Northamptonshire home which their father took over when he became the eighth Earl Spencer in June 1975.

They also spent time with their grandmother, Ruth Fermoy, who passed on to them her great love of music. Lady Fermoy was the founder of the King's Lynn Festival to which she attracted some of Britain's finest musicians, and every summer she made sure that her grandchildren came to at least one of her concerts there in the medieval Guildhall of St George.

It had been Diana's ambition from an early age to be a ballet dancer, but at West Heath she discovered she was growing too tall, and changed to tap dancing instead. Long hours of practice in the Park House pool paid dividends at the school swimming sports, where she carried off more than her fair share of trophies.

'When she dived,' remembers her headmistress, 'you never heard a splash.'

She involved herself cheerfully in social service, visiting the elderly and playing with handicapped children once a week, and when she left West Heath, at the end of 1977, she was given a special award for service.

'We don't give this every year,' explained the headmistress in 1981, a little nonplussed that Earl Spencer's less-than-academic daughter had suddenly become West Heath's most famous Old Girl. 'It's presented only to outstanding pupils,' and from an otherwise undisclosed school report were extracted the encouraging words: 'She's a girl who notices what needs to be done, then does it willingly and cheerfully.'

One weekend in her final term at West Heath, Lady Diana got special permission to go home for the weekend. There was to be a shoot at Althorp over the fields that had been fresh turned since the harvest, and the guest of honour was the Prince of Wales, who was at that time going out with Lady Sarah, the oldest of the Spencer girls.

'But it was obvious,' remembers her father, 'that it was Diana who was occupying his attentions. Somehow she automatically ended up standing at the side of Prince Charles.'

If the Prince and Princess had not themselves recalled that meeting in November 1977 so vividly, one might be tempted to dismiss the Earl's recollection as a fond father's rearrangement of history. But that freshturned field clearly stuck in their minds, and others who saw the couple together then now look back and see special significance in the bounciness of the jolly, amusing and attractive sixteen-year-old who found Prince Charles 'pretty amazing'. Lady Diana Spencer had met her prince, and from that point onwards the evidence of her life suggests she only had one man on her mind.

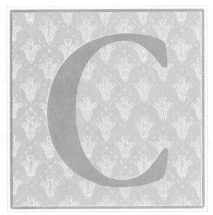

oleherne Court is a complex of red brick apartments marking some sort of frontier between the bedsitterland of Earls Court and the white stucco of the Boltons, home of grocery millionaires and Saudi sheikhs. It is a mansion block like many others, but since the spring of 1981 the more enterprising tours of London's sights have taken to including it in their itinerary, for in flat no. 60, on the corner of Block H, looking down over the public library, there lived for a period the future Queen of England.

'I remember the first time I sat outside here,' says James Whitaker. 'It was early one morning in September 1980, and I couldn't believe my luck. At 7.15 the front door opened and out came this girl, tall, slim and very, very pretty. She walked down the road to one of the Indian delicatessens, came out with some bottles of milk, bought a morning paper and then went back in for breakfast.'

The royal sleuth had stumbled upon Lady Diana Spencer starting a day like any other she had lived since she set up for herself in London in the summer of 1979. She had left West Heath soon after her meeting with Prince Charles at Althorp, and, after a term at a Swiss finishing school, she had come back to England to work. She had enrolled with an agency and got a job looking after a little American boy three days a week.

Coleherne Court, Block H

To start with she lived at her mother's home in Pimlico, but in the summer of 1979 her parents bought her an apartment in Coleherne Court, and she moved in with three friends – a china restorer, a music student and a secretary to an estate agent. Together they lived the life of well-heeled bachelor girls, sharing the cooking and cleaning, and going together to parties. Of the four, it was Diana who had most the tendency to 'tidy up' after the others. She bit her nails; she ate more sweets than were good for her; and at parties she proved well able to fend for herself: several boyfriends paid court to her, but there was never anything too intense.

'It was as if her day-to-day existence only consumed a part of her that did not matter,' says a friend, 'as if her innermost heart were elsewhere.'

Her middle sister, Jane, had married Robert Fellowes, assistant private secretary to the Queen, and this intensified her contact with the royal family. She quite frequently drove up from Coleherne Court to see her sister in Kensington Palace, where the Fellowes had a home, and when she was spotted with Prince Charles on the banks of the Dee in September 1980, one reason for her being at Balmoral was to help her sister look after her newborn baby girl.

By this time, however, the courtship was in earnest. Lady Diana had seen the Prince several times that summer. She had been his guest at Cowes on board the royal yacht *Britannia*, leaning over the rail to tweak the mast of his sailboard and send him tumbling into the Solent. Up at Balmoral the precautions taken to conceal her from the press made it clear that she was not just any other member of the royal party – and the hounds picked up the scent.

James Whitaker was the first at Coleherne Court.

'I'm looking for the Lady Diana Spencer,' he said, adopting the lordly tone in which he had frequently found himself addressed in several years of royal reporting, and the porter gave him the lady's flat number, and her telephone number as well.

For the future Princess of Wales it was the beginning of a curious relationship. In previous centuries would-be Queens of England have had to gratify spies, politicians and portrait painters dispatched to weigh up their qualities and bring back impressions by which king and country could make a judgement. In 1981 it is doorstepping reporters and cameramen that the candidate must charm – while never being so charming as to offend the people who really count. In 1978 Lady Diana's sister Sarah had once been so rash as to talk about the Prince of Wales and her friendship with him, and this interview, as it appeared in *Woman's Own*, did not impress Buckingham Palace.

In our 1980s fairy tale, press reporters and photographers can be seen as the knaves and varlets, and among them James Whitaker takes on the role of the Demon King. Before turning to matters royal, he specialized in marriage break-ups, coaxing out of Vivien Merchant the immortal comment on the departure of her husband, Harold Pinter, with the Lady Antonia Fraser: 'He didn't have to take any shoes, she has very big feet, you know'; and it was Mr Whitaker who, in November 1980, was to cajole Lady Diana Spencer's uncle, the Lord Fermoy, into discussing over the telephone whether or not his niece was a virgin. Small wonder that the lady herself had felt safest observing him with a hand mirror from behind a tree.

Running the gauntlet. Lady Diana Spencer emerges from her flat to face the press

'If you stand right back here in the darkness,' says Whitaker, in the shadow of a building facing Coleherne Court, 'you just can't be seen. The secret is not to move. That's what I tell the photographers with me. "Don't move until the last minute."'

'I remember one night she'd parked her Metro just over there. Then the photographer moved, she saw us, she jumped back into the car, and she drove off down the Little Boltons like a fighter pilot scrambling.'

Lady Diana's sister Sarah had tried to keep her relationship with her pursuers on a friendly basis in the days when she had been close to Prince Charles; she called James Whitaker 'James'. In the winter of 1980–81 her youngest sister adopted a similar approach, but she never called the *Daily Star*'s royal reporter anything other than 'Mr Whitaker'.

It was a fine display of grace under pressure. Always courteous, she and her flatmates invariably answered the door of their flat, and never put down the phone on journalists. They almost always smiled as they bore out of their front door into a fusillade of flashlights, and the lady herself, running the daily gauntlet of men practising the royal reporter's art of asking questions while walking rapidly backwards, managed to get through nearly five months of interrogation without once resorting to the cliché 'No comment'. She giggled, she smiled, she pursed her lips to look serious but then burst out laughing, and she succeeded in getting all of them to fall thoroughly in love with her.

'You fancy her,' Mrs Whitaker would shout at her husband as he clambered out of bed before dawn to take up his doorstep vigil on wintry mornings.

'Of course I fancy her,' Mr Whitaker would retort. '*Everybody* fancies her.'

She had the gift of making people feel they must look after her. She was a daughter, a girlfriend, a sister – never a mistress.

All this time she kept up her work at the patriotically named Young England kindergarten in a church hall not far from Victoria Station. With fees of £150 a term her charges were scarcely underprivileged: they included a Cabinet minister's son, one juvenile Macmillan and a playpenful of baby merchant bankers. But they got as frightened as any other kids would be at strange men trying to climb in through the lavatory window, and it was in an effort to spare her charges this harassment that Lady Diana agreed to pose for pictures in her ordinary working clothes.

'Damn fine legs,' was Prince Charles's chivalrous reaction to the spectacular consequences of her happening to have stood in a thin muslin skirt with the sunlight behind her.

It was the first time that a would-be Princess of Wales had submitted to a mass photocall, but it was becoming clear that the lady had her own way of doing things. At Ludlow races that autumn she jumped up and down with abandon, noisily encouraging Prince Charles's efforts in a steeple-chase, and she was not ashamed to have it known that she had put a bet on him – for a place.

By Christmas 1980 the couple had discussed marriage. She had made no secret of her love for him, and he, as he later admitted, was affected by this. He did not actually propose to her, but he had sounded her out on the subject of getting married in his rather cautious way, and he also took her to look round the new country home he had bought that summer in Gloucestershire, Highgrove House near Tetbury.

'You must only marry the man you love,' her father told her when she confided in him her wish to marry the Prince of Wales.

'That is what I am doing,' she replied.

The proposal itself came early in February 1981 when Prince Charles invited her for dinner in his book-cluttered blue sitting room on the left-hand side of Buckingham Palace. She was due to go to Australia for a holiday with her mother, and it seemed to the Prince that this would give her the chance to reflect on the proposition which he had to put to her. But she needed no time for reflection.

'It wasn't a difficult decision,' she said later. 'It was what I wanted – it is what I want.'

When she got back home with the news to her flatmates, the happiness knew no bounds.

'We started to squeal with excitement,' remembers one of them, 'then we burst into floods of tears.'

On 24 February 1981 the news was made public. The Lord Chamberlain, Lord Maclean, stepped forward to announce the engagement to a roomful of investiture guests at Buckingham Palace, while the Queen looked on in a rosy glow, and at the very same moment, on the dot of eleven o'clock, three policemen took up positions at the doors of Coleherne Court. Lady Diana Spencer's wedding day was five months off, but already she was regarded as being royal.

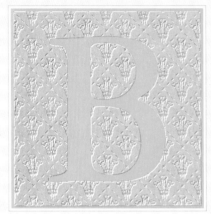

Britain surprised itself with the great outburst of joy that greeted the news of the royal engagement. It was the first unarranged marriage by a Prince of Wales in history, and the Princess-to-be was not afraid to proclaim to the world that it was a love match, even if her fiancé was more equivocal ('Whatever "in love" means,' he said). The brief minutes of interview in which they described their courtship and plans for the future were replayed so frequently on television through the day that by the late-night bulletins viewers almost knew them by heart – 'With Prince Charles beside me I can't go wrong.' It was a spontaneous and memorable moment of celebration.

There were those, of course, who declined to rejoice. Mr Willie Hamilton MP played true to his self-appointed role as wicked fairy to royal frolics by suggesting that the engagement was staged in some way to divert attention from the appalling unemployment figures – and appalling those figures certainly were. But the euphoria which greeted the news that the heir to the throne was to be married was not contrived, and the sense of communal happiness that was to grow in the coming months, in paradoxical tandem with the social frustration building up in areas like Brixton and Toxteth, was more than simple escapism.

It was in part a tribute to the character of the girl who would one day be Queen. Lady Diana Spencer was welcomed by a world grown sick of rebels and ravers, and now delighted to discover that the qualities of moderation and commonsense, so generally admired in the royal family, were alive and well and had been living in Earls Court in the custody of someone so young, pretty and eminently *balanced*. She had been tried and tested in the previous months. She had stood the test.

Help at last. Detectives take over at Coleherne Court

'What will make the marriage so good,' said her stepmother, Raine, who had married Earl Spencer in 1976, 'is that Diana is a giver.'

The arrival of Raine Spencer with the bride-to-be's father, the Earl, in the crowds outside Buckingham Palace on engagement day lent an added touch to the general jubilation. The television interviewers could scarcely conceal their astonishment.

'What are you doing *outside* the Palace?'

'Posing for the photographers,' replied the Earl happily, and immediately established himself as a hit act in his own right. Brandishing his own camera, he explained that he had taken pictures of all the other great occasions in his daughter's life, and that he was not missing out on this one. In an interview repeated through the day almost as much as his daughter's, he revealed that Prince Charles had formally asked him for permission to marry her – 'I don't know what he'd have said if I'd turned him down' – and also that she had, as a baby, been 'a superb physical specimen'.

It all proved the wisdom of J. H. Thomas, the trade-union leader and socialist politician, who had explained to Harold Nicolson the reason why Edward VIII had to abdicate in 1936: 'Now 'ere we 'ave this obstinate little man with 'is Mrs Simpson. Hit won't do, 'Arold, I tell you that straight. I know the people of this country. I *know* them. They 'ate 'aving no family life at Court.' Prince Charles and Lady Diana Spencer were now promising to renew that family life, and in the *New Statesman* Professor Sir Edmund Leach suggested, as an anthropologist, that this promise of renewal stirred feelings deep in the national subconscious.

'Both individually and nationally,' he wrote, 'we need constant reassurance that, despite the certainty of death, we are immortal. It is no good saying that it is "irrational" to believe in immortality; of course it is; but the psychological need to feel some assurance of survival goes very deep … *Le Roi est mort, vive le Roi.* Conversely, an unmarried heir to the throne is a threat to our collective immortality. Prince Charles just *had* to get married. Indeed on several occasions, long before Lady Diana was considered as a candidate, he said so himself.'

Americans were pleased to hear that Lady Diana, through her Fermoy blood, was one eighth American, and that she was related, if only distantly, to both Humphrey Bogart and Rudolph Valentino. Nigerians were intrigued by the news that the marriage would, according to the *Nigerian Sunday Times*, be consummated by the Archbishop of Canterbury and 'a team of other top clergymen'.

The *Guardian* could not resist the chance which the lady's name gave to pun, looking forward to her trying on her wedding gown, Di-namite, revealing her slimming secrets, Di-et, frowning at photographers, Di-abolical, and eventually seeing a doctor for a Di-agnosis which would, inevitably, be followed by a Di-aper. The newspaper ruminated, however, on the charms of her full name, borne by the Roman goddess of the moon, hunting and virginity: 'Always refer to Diana,' was its conclusion,

Earl Spencer in front of Althorp with Raine, his second wife

The ring – one sapphire and fourteen diamonds

precisely reflecting the feelings of the lady herself, who has been seen to wince at the excessive deployment of a nickname shunned by her family and intimates. 'Never say Di.'

It was all enormous fun. The hope and curiosity represented by the crowds of cameramen who had laid siege to Coleherne Court had become legitimate. Lady Diana Spencer now belonged to the nation, and the nation now prepared with her thoroughly to enjoy her wedding day.

avid and Elizabeth Emanuel started designing the wedding dress in the spring of 1981, when the shooting of President Reagan was fresh in everyone's mind. So they felt they had to ask whether their creation should be constructed around a bulletproof vest.

Buckingham Palace had never heard of such a thing.

The second step was to hire twenty-four-hour security guards and to instal a safe. They tried to do it discreetly, but the safe got stuck in the doorway and had, eventually, to be hoisted high above street level on a crane, then swung through a hole in the wall created by the removal of one whole window.

The couple found their waste bins were vanishing mysteriously. So, having decided upon an ivory creation, they made sure that all the snippings that went out with the rubbish were plain white. Scraps from the real dress were all religiously burned in little ceremonies at the end of each day.

'We weren't told to do it,' says Elizabeth Emanuel. 'It just seemed the thing to do.'

Two girls in the workroom knew about the design. Two others didn't, and every time they brought pins or thread into the room where the work was going on, they would walk in with faces averted and arms outstretched.

The Emanuels' fitting room is a cosy little first-floor parlour overlooking Brook Street. There is a long window seat scattered with moiré cushions, a vase of paper roses, a blow heater on the wall. This is where Lady Diana came with her mother and bridesmaids for the pre-wedding fittings. David Emanuel had to go down to the Palace mews to measure up the coaches to make sure the dress could be manoeuvred in and out of them – and also that it left some room at least for the bride's escorts.

'Lord Spencer,' says David Emanuel respectfully, 'is a big man.'

Was there ever so much fuss about a dress? Lady journalists phoned in tears, claiming they had been threatened with the sack if they did not get the details. One paper published a story that the Emanuels were, in fact, producing three wedding dresses, so that if one were stolen or pirated, another could take its place. It was too helpful a fabrication to deny. Sightseeing coaches drove past hooting and waving. The phones scarcely stopped ringing for four months. Three PR ladies gave way under the strain. And downstairs, outside the door, the camera crews lay in wait for days on end....

Britain had a royal summer on its hands. The Emanuels, shut off from the world like atomic scientists as they laboured over their secret creation, were part of a flight of fancy on a national scale. Shops broke out in a rash of souvenirs – beer, biscuits, tea and T-shirts (though they were frowned on), all could be purchased bearing the image of the happy couple – and it became the smart thing for Mini Metro owners to sport a head of the future Princess in their rear window, waving a dainty hand. 'Pretty amazing' became something of a catchphrase, and her sayings on other matters were avidly collected: on the press – 'I love working with children, and I have learned to be very patient with them'; on life inside Buckingham Palace – 'Not too bad. But too many formal dinners (yuk!).'

She was a craze. Her hairstyle was scrutinized closely and it was discovered that she had for some time been going to her sister's hairdresser, Mr Kevin Shanley, a promising young crimper of Headlines in South Kensington. She had been having highlights put in to lighten her natural mouse – while having her eyelashes dyed darker – and she had had more highlights put in since her engagement. *Tatler* ran a feature to show how ordinary girls could make themselves look more like her, and several national newspapers ran Lady Di Lookalike competitions.

Major Ralph Rochester, of Maltfield in Devon, felt moved to write to *The Times*: 'Sir, I have observed of late numerous girls who are taking pains to look like Lady Diana; but of the boys I have observed, none is making the least effort to look like the Prince of Wales. How should this be?'

No one came forward with an answer, but a poll conducted by *National Student* magazine confirmed the accuracy of the major's observation: while virtually none of the female students polled said that they would take up the chance to marry Prince Charles, were it offered to them, one third of the men said that they found Lady Diana attractive.

It was clear that the royal family had acquired a most valuable new asset. Accomplished and charming though young royals like the Princes Charles and Andrew might be, they were almost too smooth: quirkiness and spontaneity had been polished out of them by their meticulous royal upbringing. This new recruit had chirpiness and originality. 'Diana will keep me young,' said Prince Charles, and youth was not all that she brought to their marriage.

James Whitaker, now billed by his paper as 'the man who always knew', went so far as to suggest that the Prince of Wales would have suffered a

Mother of the bride. Mrs Shand Kydd (left) after a wedding rehearsal at St Paul's

severe loss of popularity if he had not married this delightful child. 'People had got so fond of her, they'd have turned against him if he'd let her go like all the others. I remember we were waiting outside Fenwicks once while she was shopping there, and when we told the traffic wardens who the car belonged to, they went all soppy. "Ooh, that lovely girl!" they said.'

Down in Australia Anthony Holden, prince of Prince-watchers, made another interesting observation. The Prince of Wales had gone there in April on a previously arranged tour, and at first sight HRH seemed to be carrying out his duties with his customary ease: 'Wherever I go in the world, I find trees planted by my parents before me, and I notice that while my mother's seem to flourish, my father's tend to droop rather wearily. This leads me to assume that trees must be snobs.'

But Holden felt that something was wrong. The man seemed nervous, miserable even. He had been publicly engaged for nearly two months and his fiancée had been so unreserved as to cry when she said goodbye to him at London Airport, in noticeable contrast to the nonchalance with which HRH had walked up the boarding steps.

Prince Charles had not previously betrayed much tendency to lovesickness. His grudging comment on engagement day, 'Whatever "in love" means', was of a piece with his previous declarations on the subject of marriage. 'If I'm deciding on whom I want to live with for fifty years,' he had said in 1972, 'well, that's the last decision on which I would want my head to be ruled by my heart,' and he had seemed at the beginning of the engagement to have embarked upon the enterprise with one pair of fingers firmly crossed, hoping that love would flourish in conditions which appeared to be very promising.

Love, it seemed to Anthony Holden, started to flourish in Australia. Every day the papers were full of the Princess-to-be, the smart clothes she had worn, the funny things she had said, her style, her magic. 'Lady Di' was the subject of everyone's first question to him.

June 1981. Lady Diana Spencer at Royal Ascot

'Suddenly he seemed to realize,' says Holden, 'that he had got himself a winner.'

For more than a month, Prince Charles studied his fiancée as the rest of the world studied her, through the adoring blitz of newspapers, magazines and television, and he came to the same conclusion as the world did.

'It was an extreme case of absence making the heart grow fonder. He fell in love with her just like Joe Public.'

Back in Buckingham Palace the Queen's press secretary, Michael Shea, found himself the object of extraordinary blandishments. The major American television networks were bringing massive teams to London, and they all wanted interviews with just one person. Could Tom Brokaw speak to her, could Dan Rather, could Barbara Walters? These high priests of the tube, who ration their blessings only grudgingly to presidents and potentates, were not out in the streets of Brixton or Toxteth investigating the pressures that were to explode that summer in the most bitter and destructive rioting Britain had experienced in a century. They were paying court to the Palace, almost literally on their knees, begging for just a few minutes with this girl, less than half their age, whose principal achievement hitherto had been to spend a few months looking after children in a kindergarten.

 uckingham Palace, July 1981. It is a wet afternoon and 2000 guests are standing out in the garden, trying not to think too hard about the damp seeping up through their shoes.

'Do you think she'll come out if it stays like this?' asks one lady, peering up at the sky through the jungle of umbrellas. But as the royal family start down those steps on which the famous engagement pose was struck, Lady Diana Spencer appears unflustered by the elements. The rain is dripping off her hat.

'I shall sit down and sulk if it's like this in Gibraltar,' she says with a giggle. 'There'll be no rain left at this rate.'

In six days' time she will be a princess, and several guests wish her well. Many of them are disabled, and when she realizes that one elderly lady is blind, she extends her left hand.

'Do you want to feel my engagement ring?' she asks. 'I'd better not lose it before Wednesday, or they won't know who I am.'

Weeks previously this girl was no more royal than these onlookers now craning to snatch a passing glimpse of her, and she takes on a conspiratorial air as she lets them in on a few secrets of her new eminence.

'We had a wedding rehearsal yesterday,' she tells one group, bending forward. 'Everybody was fighting. I got my heel stuck in some grating and everyone was saying "Hurry up, Diana." I said, "I can't. I'm stuck."'

She rolls her eyes, and pulls faces that she must have learnt in the dorm at Riddlesworth Hall.

Prince Charles is a few yards behind her, slightly hoarse and sucking a cough sweet on the afternoon after the night before, his stag night.

'If he comes past,' she says, pointing backwards, 'ask him why he's looking so pale.'

She has worked out a beguiling routine with the carnations and roses that people press upon her. She slips them into the buttonholes of guests farther down the line, and this makes grown men blush like schoolboys. One gets himself into a frightful muddle.

'Will you be watching the wedding?' she asks him.

'Yes,' he replies. 'Will you?' – then looks crestfallen as he realizes what he has said.

The wink she gives him makes his mortification a million times worthwhile.

'I'm in it,' she giggles.

The wedding is the principal topic of conversation, if that is the word for the exchanges with which she zigzags to and fro, taking more than an hour to cover the 400 yards to the tea tent.

'You'll be watching *all day?*' she asks. 'You'll get a huge electricity bill!'

'Good luck, Diana!' shouts someone who cannot shoulder his way to the front, but who is clearly unwilling to go home without having conveyed his sentiments to the lady.

'I don't know if I'll be able to remember what went on, or if I'll just be in a haze,' she says, 'so I'm going to videotape it. Then I'll be able to run back over the best bits – and when it comes to the part that says "I will", I'm going to take that out and put in something else.'

ad she married any other well-born young naval officer, she could probably have counted upon some pictures in the social pages. Marrying the heir to the throne of England made her great day an occasion for the whole world. Photographers flew from every corner of the globe to compile wedding albums which were, in the weeks to come, to sell in tens of millions of copies – and several more ribald compilations also did good business. *Private Eye* produced *Born to be Queen*, 'Not the Nine o'Clock News' published *Not the Royal Wedding*, and Clive James gathered some heavy antipodean jests in *Charles Charming's Challenges on the Pathway to the Throne*, all three books joking naughtily about the bride's relatives and the bridegroom's ears – saucy wedding-breakfast telegrams from the nation.

On the night before the wedding, BBC and Independent Television had combined to present an interview with the happy couple. They were filmed in the summerhouse at Buckingham Palace and the collapsible canvas chairs in which they were set accentuated her tendency to hunch her shoulders downwards. There were to be fireworks that night in Hyde Park which Prince Charles would be attending. Would Lady Diana be there as well?

No. She hoped to be 'tucked up in bed' early in Clarence House. 'We're not allowed to see each other the night before – we might quarrel.'

Had Prince Charles been a great help in the recent months?

Lady Diana: 'Marvellous, oh, a tower of strength.'

HRH: 'Gracious!'

Lady Diana: 'I had to say that because you're sitting there.'

Celebrants had gathered days before, among the earliest a Mr Stephen Tinsley, who took up his position on the Mall seventy-two hours ahead of time. On the Monday before the wedding it became clear that Mr Tinsley could have spent an extra twenty-four hours at home and still have secured his place, but, resplendent in a Union Jack T-shirt, he had no regrets.

'If you are going to be a fanatic,' he said, 'you might as well do a good job of it.'

That turned out to be an appropriate theme for the entire day – 'the sort of thing,' remarked the *Sunday Times* afterwards, 'that we overdo so well.'

In Clarence House, the bride was watching television, following the progress of the early processions and preparations. Kevin Shanley, the confectioner of her famous hairstyle, was with her, hard at work modifying her fringe to the requirements of tiara and veil.

Barbara Daly, the make-up artist (normal fee for a wedding £150 – plus VAT), had already set up her table of paints and powders. Her intention, she had said, was to keep the make-up light – 'Lady Diana naturally blushes very prettily, and there's no point pretending she doesn't.'

The master of ceremonies for the great day was Lord Maclean, the Lord Chamberlain, and when, some time around ten, the guests in St Paul's Cathedral saw him take the two halves of his wand of office and screw them together as if assembling a billiard cue, they knew that the fun was about to begin. Commentators made much of the fact that St Paul's in pre-Christian times was, by tradition, the site of a temple to Diana; less classically inclined reporters resorted to nursery Hollywood, as they described the bride approaching 'the church on the hill'.

The family provided a fashion parade in their own right – the Queen in aquamarine silk crepe-de-Chine, the Queen Mother in green silk georgette, Princess Margaret in coral, Mrs Shand Kydd in hyacinth blue. Opinions were divided on Princess Anne's white and yellow outfit: some thought it the height of chic, but one French newspaper averred she looked like an *omelette Norvègienne* (a Norwegian omelette is a dollop of cold ice cream dropped on top of hot beaten eggs).

Liz Emanuel's vision had been that the bride should emerge from her carriage like a butterfly breaking out of its chrysalis, and so it proved as the bridesmaids hurried round Lady Diana, plucking out and straightening the acres of crushed ivory silk taffeta and lace embroidered with mother-of-pearl sequins and pearls.

The 'old' was the lace – it had once belonged to Queen Mary; the 'new' was the silk, the work of British silkworms which had been munching down in Dorset for months on twenty sacks of mulberry leaves a day; the 'borrowed' was her tiara, a family heirloom, together with her diamond earrings, which belonged to her mother; the 'blue' was a tiny bow of ribbon sewn into the waistband, with a horseshoe of 18-carat yellow gold sewn in beside it. A group of lacemakers claimed that they had provided a blue garter to grace the soon-to-be-royal thigh, but this was one sartorial detail on which Buckingham Palace preserved an unwavering 'No comment'.

Her appearance as she walked up the cathedral steps to the cheers of the crowd more than justified the verse composed in her honour by the President of Zimbabwe, the Rev. Canaan Banana:

> *It was worth waiting for the one most fitting*
> *It was worth sweating for the one most soothing*
> *It was worth living for the one most loving.*

(President Banana was due to hold political discussions while in London, and officials of the Zimbabwe news agency had been instructed that they should on no account describe these talks as 'fruitful'.)

'The Trumpet Voluntary' sounded; it was time for the bride to start her procession down the aisle, and it seemed less that she was on the arm of her father, Earl Spencer, than that he, shaky after the stroke he suffered in 1977, was drawing strength from the tall, triumphant daughter beside him. Her prince stood waiting for her beneath the great arch of the cathedral dome.

'Dearly beloved,' intoned the Dean of St Paul's, and the marriage service had begun. It was relayed by loudspeakers to the crowds outside, and as the couple pledged themselves to one another, great roars rang out. When the bride said, 'I will,' the whole cathedral seemed to shake with the vast joy outside and, as she heard the roar, Lady Diana smiled.

There are parts of the world, said the Archbishop of Canterbury, where brides and grooms wear crowns on their wedding day to show that they have become kings and queens of creation.

'We as human beings can help shape this world,' was his message. 'We are not victims.'

She muddled up her husband's names and he, by mistake, left out the word 'worldly' and promised to share all *her* goods with her.

'*That* was no mistake,' said Princess Anne, watching it all played back on television that evening.

'I pronounce that they be man and wife together,' declared the Archbishop. Lady Diana Spencer was now the Princess of Wales.

Outside Buckingham Palace the crowds were listening on their radios, and at the Archbishop's words they rose to their feet and cheered.

'What's happening?' inquired Jane Pauley of NBC TV, sitting on a wooden platform above their heads. 'Has her blood turned blue or something?'

NBC had gathered a glittering array of local experts on their platform by the Palace to sustain seven hours of continuous television: Peter Ustinov, Michael Caine, Lady Longford, Germaine Greer and Sir Huw Weldon, complete with a balsawood model to show what was going on behind the scenes. Each of the US networks had waved their chequebooks vigorously to corral competing celebrities, and these guests leaned on the scaffolding, gossiping with friends on neighbouring platforms about their transatlantic hosts.

'Twenty years' journalistic experience,' called Nigel Dempster from the ABC raft, 'just to say, "The bride looks radiant."'

The whole scene, said Peter Ustinov, was somehow reminiscent of the yachts moored side by side in Cannes harbour.

Back inside the cathedral the last hymn of the service was being sung. It was the one that she had chosen, 'I Vow to Thee My Country', that anthem blessed with the rare ability to kindle enthusiasm in school assemblies, and when it was finished she went to sign the register.

Settling down in her open carriage outside the cathedral she felt, or perhaps she allowed herself to feel, for the first time, the full warmth of the crowd's adoration, and she raised both her hands in the air to wave. Then she remembered herself.

The Emanuels were waiting inside the Palace ready to titivate the costumes for the photographs of bride and family.

Princess of Wales. The bride and groom leave St Paul's, 29 July 1981

'It was like being at any other wedding, with faces around that you've known all your life. It was difficult to remember that the Queen and the Duke did not know *us*, and that we couldn't just go up and say, "Well, how are you then?"'

BBC 2 had devoted its transmissions for the day to a presentation of the festivities, with subtitles for deaf viewers, and it was some of them who claimed to lipread what the Princess said to her husband as they stood together side by side on the Palace balcony.

She: 'They want us to kiss.'

He: 'Why not?'

So she kissed him.

Her new brothers-in-law gave her quite a homely send off. The ball given by the Queen two nights before the wedding had been decorated with clouds of heart-shaped blue and silver balloons emblazoned with the Prince of Wales's feathers – revellers had left the Palace gates in the small hours waving them enthusiastically – and the Princes Andrew and Edward secreted a supply to tie behind the honeymoon carriage; they also scrawled 'Just Married' on the back, using a stick of lipstick purloined from a lady-in-waiting. Everyone admired the new Princess's jaunty going-away outfit, in cantaloup silk, and the sharp-eyed noticed that she was now wearing the same six-strand pearl choker that her sister Sarah had been wearing at the cathedral – and that her sister went home bare-necked.

They were late for their train at Waterloo, but it waited. There were still rose petals on her dress as she got into the train, and virtually the last thing she did before she left was to plant a kiss on the cheek of Lord Maclean, who had helped make her day so memorable.

'It was a lovely surprise,' he said when questioned afterwards about this unscheduled item on the agenda, and as he spoke, it seemed to some that the Lord Chamberlain's cheek turned just a little pinker.

That evening the family celebrated at Claridges. Patrick Lichfield's sister, Lady Elizabeth Shakerley, gave a party, and everybody was there: the Queen, Prince Philip, Prince Andrew, Prince Edward, Princess Margaret and Lord Snowdon (separately, his Lordship being accompanied by his new wife Lucy), the young Snowdons, Princess Anne and Mark Phillips, Princess Alexandra. There were royals to the nth degree, and the hotel seemed to have become an overflow annex for Buckingham Palace. David Frost found himself talking to a nice old gentleman who turned out to be King Olav of Norway.

Mrs Reagan was there, accompanied by several heavily built men with watchful eyes, and so was Princess Grace of Monaco. Prince Philip danced a lot with her. The band had been flown in from New York and when they were off duty everyone kept confusing their bulky black saxophonist with the King of Tonga. He could scarcely move for people bowing and calling him 'Your Majesty'.

Large video screens had been set up so that people could enjoy the day all over again, and that provided an unexpected bonus for the guests – the spectacle of Queen Elizabeth II watching herself on television while drinking a dry martini and pointing delightedly whenever the cameras caught one of her famous glum faces.

Prince Andrew thought it a great joke when the bride muddled up the names of her intended.

'She's just married my father,' he said.

It was noticed that the Queen beamed with pleasure every time her new daughter-in-law came up on the screen, and all agreed that the happiness and informality of the occasion owed much to the young lady who was not present.

The foyer was decorated with silver birch sprayed blue, the ballroom with real green apples hanging from a canopy of maypole ribbons. There was *grand marque* champagne to drink all night, and high-class breakfast food, scrambled eggs, kedgeree, bacon, salmon fishcakes and lots of fresh summer fruit – because, explained the hostess, she could not afford caviar and lobster.

The dancing went on past four in the morning, and it was 1.30 before Elizabeth II went home – late for her. For most of the evening Prince Philip had been wearing a saucy boater which said 'Charles and Diana' on the hatband, and it was only with great difficulty that Her Majesty prevailed upon her husband to take it off before he walked outside.

'I'd love to stay and dance all night,' said the Queen as she left – and she hitched up the hem of her skirt and did a little jig just to show that she meant it.

THE ENGAGEMENT

*Lady Diana Spencer
with two of the children she
looked after at the Young
England kindergarten,
Pimlico. Hoping to raise the
press siege which was worrying
the children, she agreed to pose
for photographers in
September 1980*

Grace under pressure. The future Princess of Wales keeps on with her work as the world's press pursues her through the streets of London

33

*A*n ambush at every corner. The press discovered Lady Diana Spencer's friendship with the Prince of Wales early in September 1980. Their engagement was not announced until the end of February 1981, so for nearly

six months she had to survive constant curiosity going out for the night (left), leaving a party (centre), or just taking a trip to the shops (right). She tried to pretend the cameras were not there, but sometimes she could not help looking

*T*hat dress. The engagement of the Prince of Wales to Lady Diana Spencer was announced on 24 February 1981, and on 9 March the couple attended their first formal evening engagement together, at the Goldsmiths' Hall in the City of London. Among the guests was Princess Grace of Monaco (below)

*T*he Privy Council
approved the forthcoming
marriage on 27 March 1981,
and the couple were
photographed with the Queen
in Buckingham Palace (right).
Earlier that day they had been
in Cheltenham (this page).
'May I kiss the hand of my
future Queen?' asked
Nicholas Hardy, an eighteen-
year-old schoolboy, proffering
one golden daffodil from the
far side of a police barricade.
Lady Diana, who had landed
at Dean Close School only
moments before in a helicopter
piloted by her betrothed, took
the flower, considered the
proposition, and smiled prettily.
'Yes, you may,' she said,
extending her hand.
Nicholas kissed, the schoolboys
laughed, and the queen-to-be
giggled.
'You will never live this
down,' she said

*F*acing forward. Lady Diana Spencer at Broadlands, home of the late Lord Mountbatten, where she
went with Prince Charles on 9 May 1981 to open an exhibition in honour of the Prince's 'honorary grandfather'

Welcome to the village. The inhabitants of Tetbury, Gloucestershire, welcome Lady Diana Spencer on 22 May 1981 (this page and following). She came to inspect the local hospital, and also her new home just down the road, Highgrove House, where she and the Prince were to take up residence a few months later

*L*eisure wear. *Lady Diana relaxes in dungarees and jeans (left and right), and in
more formal wear (centre), when the Prince stops off at Smiths Lawn for a game on his way home from Ascot*

*F*amily occasion.
On 4 June 1981 Lady Diana
Spencer accompanied Prince
Charles, Princess Margaret
and Queen Elizabeth the
Queen Mother to the wedding
of Prince Charles's friend,
Nicholas Soames.
Prince Charles was best man

*R*oyal enclosure.
Lady Diana Spencer is the
centre of attention at Royal
Ascot in June 1981

*L*ady's Day.
Heads turn for Lady Diana
Spencer at Ascot with Prince
Charles and (above) with
Princess Alexandra

*W*eeping Beauty.
On 24 June 1981 Lady Diana
Spencer accompanied the
Prince of Wales to the gala
premiere of the film For Your
Eyes Only *at the Odeon,*
Leicester Square, in aid of the
National Society for the
Prevention of Cruelty to
Children and the Royal
Association for Disability and
Rehabilitation (right). She
sparkled in a flowing gown.
But there were other occasions
(left) when the strain of
constant attention told

*A kiss for the Queen.
Lady Diana Spencer greets her
mother-in-law-to-be at
Smiths Lawn, Windsor, on 26
July 1981 (right), a few days
before the wedding. The
newspapers kept saying that
she found polo a bore, but she
watched a great deal of polo in
the summer of her engagement
(above and left), and she gave
every sign of enjoying herself
thoroughly. Overleaf, she
applauds at Wimbledon*

THE WEDDING

*T*he kiss.
'*They want us to kiss,*' *she said.*
'*Why not?*' *he replied. So they did, and the whole world cheered.*
On previous pages, St Paul's Cathedral and the ride back to Buckingham Palace

*I*t really doesn't
matter if you suck your
thumb . . .
The bride reassures her
youngest bridesmaid,
Clementine Hambro, before
the photographs start inside
Buckingham Palace – and the
Queen adds a comforting
word as well

*S*o I said
to the Archbishop ... Prince
Charles amuses his bride and
his brothers Prince Edward
and Prince Andrew (left and
far left) after the formal
photographs are over. The
bride's attendants, from left to
right, were Edward van
Cutsem, Clementine
Hambro, Catherine
Cameron, India Hicks, Sarah
Jane Gasalee, Lady Sarah
Armstrong-Jones and Lord
Nicholas Windsor, the son of
the Duke and Duchess of
Kent.
Overleaf, the couple leave for
their honeymoon, balloons
courtesy of Princes Andrew
and Edward

THE HONEYMOON

*Going away.
The new Princess
waves as she
boards the train
at Waterloo
Station on her
wedding day
(left). A few days
later she flew
with her husband
from
Southampton
(right), having
started her
honeymoon, as
his parents did, at
Broadlands, the
home of the
late Lord
Mountbatten*

*A*lone at last.
The Prince and Princess of Wales on board the royal yacht Britannia *as it steams out into the Mediterranean from Gibraltar on Saturday, 2 August 1981*

The honeymooners set off first for the islands of the Aegean Sea (top left), where they succeeded in enjoying some swimming and sunbathing on deserted islands and beaches. Then the royal yacht sailed on to the eastern

Mediterranean to disembark at Port Said (top right and lower left) where they were received in state by Egypt's President Sadat and his wife. Britannia *sailed on southwards down the Suez Canal into the Red Sea*

*E*ast of Suez.
The Princess revelled in the
heat of Egypt in mid-August.
She wore a hat to protect her
hair, but when she got home
her highlights were noticeably
blonder. She had also acquired
a deep tan.
'We look like a couple of black
and white minstrels,' she said
on 15 August 1981, as she got
off the plane back in Scotland
with her husband

*D*eeside.
They had first been spotted together early in September 1980 on the banks of the River Dee. Now, less than a year later, on 19 August 1981, they appeared openly together to be photographed, a young couple just married and very much in love

*P*hotocall.
They could have been fashion models, going through their paces for the assembled photographers. He wore the Balmoral tartan. She wore a hound's-tooth check suit designed and made up for her by Bill Pashley, her mother's Battersea dressmaker. On Saturday, 5 September 1981, the Prince and Princess visited the Highland Games at Braemar (overleaf)

PRINCESS OF WALES

Welcome to Wales. Pouring rain could not dampen the enthusiasm with which the Princess was received by the people of Wales on her tour from 27 to 29 October 1981, nor did she allow her umbrella to get in the way of her contact with the crowds. Children chanted her name wherever she appeared, hoping to persuade her to walk in their direction – and usually they succeeded

*R*ed and Green.
*The Princess chose the colours
of Wales to wear on her visit
to Caernarvon, the site of her
husband's investiture in 1969.
Her suit was a new one, from
the London dressmaker
Donald Campbell, but the hat
was the one she had worn to
the Soames wedding four
months previously (see page
48), with green on the band.
Her hatmaker, John Boyd,
was of the opinion she wore his
creation too far back on her
head while she was in Wales.
'The secret of hat-wearing lies
in the angle you set it at. Still,
she's learning – and she looks
lovely anyway, bless her heart'*

*G*od bless the Princess of Wales. The market
town of Brecon turned out in force on 29 October 1981 to
cheer Wales's first Princess for more than seventy years

*F*reedom of the City. In Swansea the Princess attended a special gala of Welsh music and dance (this page). In Cardiff (right) she was given the Freedom of the City, swearing an oath to be obedient to the Lord Mayor and to 'Obey his Warrants, Precepts and Commands'. She was presented with a scroll in a silver casket which, by unanimous resolution of the city's seventy-five councillors, declared her to be 'a person of distinction'

*S*tate Opening.
*Peers who had not taken up
their seats in years made sure
they were in the House of
Lords on 4 November 1981
when the Princess of Wales,
now a member of the royal
family, attended the State
Opening of Parliament for the
first time*

*R*enaissance beauty.
On the evening of 4 November
1981 the Princess went to the
Victoria and Albert Museum
to attend the opening of the
exhibition celebrating the
Renaissance lords of Mantua,
'Splendours of the Gonzaga'
(this page and following)

*L*ighting-up time.
On 12 November 1981, the Princess visited Chesterfield
(top) and on the 20th she went back home to
Northamptonshire to open a new mail-sorting centre
(near right).
On Wednesday, the 18th, she was in London to switch
on the Christmas illuminations in Regent Street (far
right). Among the other guests was the singer Cilla
Black with her husband.
'I've brought my old man with me,' said Cilla.
'Where's yours?'
'I've left him at home,' replied the Princess, 'watching
the telly'
Previous page, the Cenotaph. On Sunday, 8 November
1981, the Princess attended the Service of
Remembrance, with King Olav of Norway, Princess
Alice, Duchess of Gloucester, and HM Queen Elizabeth
the Queen Mother

Spadework.
On 19 November 1981 the
new Princess planted a tree in .
Hyde Park commemorating
her wedding year

*S*now
Princess. She wore
cossack attire for a
service at Gloucester
Cathedral on Sunday,
13 December 1981
(right). Leaving the
Royal Opera House,
Covent Garden, she
wore more fur (left).
Overleaf, the Princess
leaving the Chapel at
Windsor on
Christmas Day

HER ROYAL HIGHNESS

snowy day at Buckingham Palace. Strange groups of men are being shepherded down the plum and gold corridor off the forecourt, all of them in their very best suits. They range in age from the late thirties to the mid-sixties. Their attempts at bonhomie indicate that they have something in common, but that they do not really know each other very well – while a certain atmosphere of unease suggests that they may be a good deal more overawed to find themselves invited inside the portals of Buckingham Palace than they are all pretending.

Now they are being shown into a grand and high-ceilinged chamber of the sort in which peace treaties are signed. Down the centre runs a highly polished long table, and in front of each chair is a silver ashtray and a notepad. Fleet Street's editors, the lords of the Fourth Estate, have been summoned to Buckingham Palace for only the second time in history, and they do not seem in the slightest dismayed when the Queen's press secretary, Michael Shea, informs them that their conclave has been convoked to discuss a twenty-year-old girl who lacks the formal qualifications to be a secretary to any one of them.

Mr Shea explains the Princess's problem – she was not born royal. Members of the royal family are trained from birth to tolerate the intensity of public scrutiny and the limitations on personal freedom which are the price of their position. But the new Princess is different, and now, bearing a potential heir to the British throne, she is feeling the strain.

The editors listen seriously. The editor of *The Times* fills most of his pad with notes. The editor of the *Sunday Express* uses only one sheet, executing a neat little drawing of a house. The editor of the *News of the World*, who is sporting a black eye, wants to know 'the facts': is the Princess heading for a nervous breakdown, is there a risk of miscarriage, is the word 'trauma' appropriate? Mr Shea tries to explain that the problem is more subtle than that.

When the talking is over, all shuffle through to another gilded chamber, lit by the same grey winter light reflected off the snow. It is warmed by a two-bar electric fire, and there the company is joined by a shortish lady in a lime green dress, carrying a very large handbag on one arm. She is recognized instantly by one and all.

'As good as the Ritz,' says the editor of the *Daily Telegraph*, complimenting Her Majesty on the dry martinis being dispensed by footmen from silver trays.

The Queen confides in the editor of the *Daily Mirror* that she is having great difficulty learning to operate her new video machine. She often has to call in one of her clever younger sons to press the right knob. Then the conversation turns to the geriatric leaders currently dominating the international scene, and the suggestion is made that the peace of the world depends upon the efficacy of monkey glands – in Mr Brezhnev's case, at least.

'They don't seem to be doing him much good,' remarks the Queen.

The *News of the World*'s editor is still worrying at his bone. 'It's very difficult,' he says, 'drawing the line between public and private. I mean, when she's out at the shops she's in public. Why shouldn't she be photographed?'

'All she wants to do,' says the young lady's mother-in-law, 'is to buy some winegums without being disturbed.'

'If she wants to buy winegums, she should send a servant to get them.'

'That,' says the Queen, 'is an extremely pompous remark, if I may say so.'

Prince Andrew is there. So is the Queen's private secretary, Sir Philip Moore, and her deputy private secretary, Mr (now Sir) William Heseltine.

'She's very young,' says the Queen. 'She's not like the rest of us.'

The meeting, and its subject, clearly have the highest priority, and the editors respond in kind. Next day their editorials preach a common line: there will be more temperance, less intrusion, fewer long lenses tracking the girl the next time she visits a sweetshop.

Their unanimity is remarkable, and so is the speed and thoroughness with which the word is passed on to their gumbooted sleuths. The time has come for restraint. Her Royal Highness the Princess of Wales has been duly certified a national treasure.

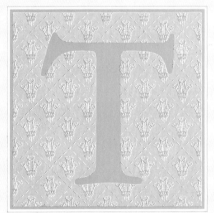

The expectation had been that, once the wedding was over, things would quieten down a bit. Britain had worked itself up into such a lather in the course of its right royal summer that it scarcely seemed possible that Lady Di fever could be sustained.

But when she got back from her honeymoon it became plain that the condition was terminal. The Greek Navy had astonished the world – and rather rattled the Turks – by most efficiently keeping the horizon between chartered flotillas of long-lens men and the *Britannia* as the royal yacht meandered romantically in the Aegean. But back in Balmoral the siege was resumed with more intensity than ever.

If ever a man and woman had been respectably married in the sight of all the world it was the Prince and Princess of Wales, but their pursuers stalked them through the heather with all the tenacity of private detectives tracking a couple on an illicit weekend, and within days it became evident that some compromise must be reached – a full-scale photo session in return for a little peace and quiet. So on Wednesday,

Honeymoon photocall.
19 August 1981 on the banks
of the River Dee

19 August 1981, the Prince and Princess went through their paces, he in a kilt, she in a skirt that was somewhat longer, in front of a battery of photographic equipment lined up on the banks of the Dee. The thunder of the stampeding motor-winds, running through film by the spoolful, only needed bugles to make it sound like a cavalry charge: clearly the world was not going to give up on the new Princess of Wales.

It was up in Scotland that the strain of it started to tell. The plot of the play *Her Royal Highness?* had been built around precisely this situation: the stage princess is told that she cannot pop out to the shops for sweets, that she cannot go round to drop in casually on her old flatmates, that all the freedoms to which she was accustomed as an ordinary mortal are now denied her – and she cracks; she runs away and, in desperation, the palace replaces her with the winner of a Lady Di Lookalike contest, a Sydney barmaid (played by the same actress), whose vocabulary consists principally of four-letter words and who drains every glass offered her at a gulp. Tragedy is thus transformed into farce.

No such remedy was available to the real Princess – but she did have powerful supporters on her side. Prince Philip's eyes would light up at the sight of her. He would really sparkle in her presence, and she had already established a close and warm relationship with her mother-in-law. If she had any problems she would go straight in to the Queen, tell her all about it and sit down for a jolly good chat – hence the summoning of the editors to Buckingham Palace. Queen Elizabeth II was very happy to give her daughter-in-law a helping hand – not least because the new Princess had already demonstrated an impressive ability to take care of herself.

Her great triumph came in Wales. Any pretty young bride should charm the world on her wedding day. But it was a more formidable proposition for a coltish scion of the English aristocracy to cast her enchantment over the valleys, the drab and coal-scarred bedrock of British socialism, home of working-class heroes like Aneurin Bevan, where unemployment at the end of October 1981, the moment of her tour, was touching 16 per cent. Welsh nationalists had prepared demonstrations – 'Go home English Princess' was their slogan – and the 'Sons of Snowdonia' had sent threatening letters to the BBC. It was, to use one of her favoured phrases, 'a great challenge' – and she rose to it magnificently.

'Seasoned analysts of the Welsh psyche,' wrote Tom Davies, reporting her tour for the *Observer*, 'are having trouble sorting out why the Welsh have fallen so abjectly and hopelessly in love with Princess Diana. For three days and 400 miles last week there was the astonishing sight of a whole nation having a nervous breakdown on rainswept pavements. Choirs sang, harps tinkled forth and grown men cried. One old man in St David's cried, pulled himself together and burst out crying again.'

Has any Englishwoman ever received such a welcome in the hillsides? She was given the freedom of the city of Cardiff, only the second female to have received it (the first was the Queen), and all the hostile demonstrations fell miserably flat. Loyal crowds jeered at the troublemakers, and the Princess herself displayed a touching inability to tell who was for her and who against. She smiled at everyone – indeed the three-day progress, from the chip shops and caravans of the northern coast down to Pembrokeshire, Swansea and Cardiff in the south, was one grand eisteddfod of smiles.

Welsh television stations broadcast the tour live all day. But it seemed that most of the Welsh wanted to come out and look her over for themselves, despite the rain. Choirs of children scrubbed clean as cherubs waited for hours in the cold to serenade her, and when they gave full throat to the anthem 'God Bless the Prince of Wales', they added a new last line, 'God Bless the Princess too.'

Prince Charles seemed happily resigned.

'Diana, love, over here,' he said as he took custody of the umpteenth bouquet.

'I'm just a collector of flowers these days,' he confided later. 'I haven't got enough wives to go round.'

James Whitaker was there. Something seemed to have gone out of his life since Lady Diana was whisked to the other side of the Palace railings, but for this great occasion the *Daily Star* had given him a team to track the Princess every centimetre of her progress through the Principality, and he delivered a stern briefing to his henchmen on the eve of Day 1: 'If the people of Wales loathe you at the end of this tour, then you'll have done your job well and I'll be proud of you.'

In Pontypridd 'the man who always knew' tried to re-create something of the intimacy of the Coleherne Court days.

'I found this nice little spot for myself behind a row of housewives, and she was coming down the line talking to them. They were loving it and she was loving it. Goodness, how she adores being a Princess!

'I had this question ready, "Your Royal Highness, how are you enjoying your welcome to Wales?" And she just had to say one word, yes or no, or almost anything, and I would have got an exclusive quote I could have used as a headline – "What the Princess of Wales said to me".

'So as she came down the line I waited till she was just opposite me, and then I popped my question at the crucial moment. She was talking to the women, holding out her hand to them, and when she heard my voice she looked up and gave me her great big grin.

'"Good afternoon, Mr Whitaker," she said, just that – and then she moved on.'

On the last night in Cardiff she had to deliver her first public speech. She chose to speak a bit of Welsh and she sounded, well, like an English girl trying to speak a bit of Welsh. But her hearers were collapsed by the honour of it all. 'Speaks it like an angel, she does. Like an angel.'

This ability, remarked Tom Davies, should be of great help to her at another time 'since, as everyone knows, Welsh is the language of Heaven.'

Umpteenth bouquet.
The Princess of Wales
in Wales, October 1981

Welsh colours. The Princess on the first day of her Welsh tour, 27 October 1981

Davies, a sardonic fellow and not one of nature's monarchists, was puzzled why his fellow countrymen, a radical race, should succumb so totally to this symbol of everything that they normally resent, and he did a little research in a pub, questioning unemployed youths unwilling to go out on the street to look at the Princess in case they might get rain in their beer.

'The general agreement was that Princess Di never comes on "posh" or "above it". In Builth Wells we watched her jumping around cleaning one of her shoes on the back of her leg. This sort of behaviour makes her like "one of us", i.e. normal. If a pin was stuck in her she would indeed bleed.

'But the real key to her success must be the way she can suddenly stop smiling in a crowd and look round, for no obvious reason, with the purest terror in her eyes, as if a man in a peaked cap had just called saying he was going to turn off the electricity. Welsh women, in particular, love this air of vulnerability, and their dearest wish would be to take her home to administer many cups of tea, a mountain of well-meaning advice, and an aspirin to put her right.'

Edward Steen, reporting the tour for the *Sunday Telegraph*, was struck by the Princess's reaction to one old soldier – 'What nice shiny medals'; then to his beaming wife – 'Did you polish them for him?' Royals who have always been royal, suggested Steen, might not be aware that medals need polishing, but the Princess's small talk betrayed more practical experience. Until recently, after all, she had been washing her own jeans.

She went home with enough presents to start up her own Welsh gifte shoppe – sticks of rock, books of illuminated poems, a plastic coathanger, two armchairs, a woolly black mountain ewe and a dreamy-looking black heifer called Sandra.

'How proud I am to be Princess of such a wonderful place and of the Welsh,' she said.

Five days later she was at Westminster, testing the epithets of another category of observer.

'For the first time in seventy-one years,' wrote Hugh Noyes, parliamentary correspondent of *The Times*, 'since 1910 when the late Queen Mary attended the ceremony in a similar role, a Princess of Wales yesterday became part of the pomp and pageantry of a State Opening of Parliament. And as the tiaras of the peeresses competed with the scarlet and ermine robes of their lordships, it seemed that in a rapidly changing world here, at least, was one tradition where nothing has changed in the past three score years and ten. Every eye in the House of Lords beamed in on the Princess as she entered the Upper Chamber with Prince Charles at her side, a few respectful feet behind the Queen and Prince Philip with their little retinue of pages.

'According to those who know about such things, the Princess wore a flowing white chiffon dress topped with a satin bodice and rounded off with puffed sleeves stretching to the elbow. To the rest of us – bishops, judges, courtiers, ladies of the bedchamber, Rouge Dragon Poursuivant and even Norfolk Herald Extraordinary – she was a glamorous concoction almost beyond description, shimmering from head to toe.'

nspiring the lobby correspondent of the top people's paper to trip the light fantastic and to write fashion copy was a notable achievement – but so much of her princessly magic derives from her visual image. She has only ever given two formal interviews, and then it was her husband-to-be who did most of the talking. She delivered herself of just 432 words – which scarcely provides a substantial basis for the massive vote of confidence which the world has bestowed upon her.

Our admiration, of course, derives from other things: her freshness, her royal status, the yet more royal status awaiting her in the future, her youth, her beauty – and her dress sense. She *looks* like a princess, groomed, elegant and clad in garments which are familiar to any woman but which, somehow, have been dusted with an extra glamour; and, in an age where fortunes are made and lost by the 'look' of a product, this is a happy gift. She likes wearing good clothes – and she tremendously enjoys buying them.

At the time of her engagement one of her friends declared that Lady Diana Spencer's favourite occupation was to spend an afternoon shopping in Knightsbridge and one of the bonuses of her new life is that her pleasure is now a duty. As the newest, most gazed-at member of the royal family, she must always look her best – and as Britain's freshest representative to the world, she must also do her bit to revive British fashion in the unswinging eighties.

She learned her shopping in Knightsbridge's 'tiara triangle', a gilt-chaired jungle whose mighty oaks are Harrods and Harvey Nichols to the north and, down in the thinner southern fringes, Peter Jones on Sloane Square and the genteel snazziness of the General Trading Company, where she had her wedding list. This area is the natural preserve of the Sloane Ranger, a British archetype comparable to the preppy in America or the *16ème girl* in Paris – a female whose cast of face, way of walking and pitch of voice characterize her unmistakably as belonging to a certain social class.

The Ranger's principal item of uniform is the silk square, commonly worn over the head and knotted under the chin or, in younger generations, worn round the neck with a jaunty knot on the side. Other insignia include the black velvet jacket, the shoulder bag, the pleated skirt, low-heeled expensive shoes and driving gloves. The livery can be

Off-the-peg, over the shoulders, and looking like a princess

Casual-looking. Dungarees for polo-watching

Blouse by Emanuel. Lady Diana Spencer photographed by Lord Snowdon for Vogue *in November 1980*

purchased at Simpson's or Jaeger, and it can be seen on parade in the members' enclosure of any British racecourse on a Saturday afternoon.

There never was much danger that Lady Diana Spencer would become a punk or a mod. Her breeding and background naturally inclined her to go a-rangering. Yet when, in her mid-teens, she became fashion-conscious, she adopted only a few of the traditional totems. The long lenses outside Coleherne Court and the Young England kindergarten caught jeans, dungarees, bright Peruvian knits and knickerbockers – and only the occasional silk square knotted around the neck. Her clothes were stylish and unstuffy, and even when she resorted to the Viyella standbys she lent them a certain zest of her own.

This would seem to be the Princess's aptitude – to add her own dash to existing stereotypes. For her honeymoon photocall on the banks of the Dee she wore a hound's-tooth check suit in tweed which, with its heavy brown leather-covered buttons down the front, was almost standard country wear. But its cut made it different. It was an outfit she had ordered in Battersea from Bill Pashley, a designer working out of a terraced house, who had been making clothes for her mother for years.

Mrs Shand Kydd has been the formative influence on her daughter's dress sense, and she was her introduction to many of the designers who now supply her clothes: Bellville Sassoon, Caroline Charles, and John Boyd, the milliner who suddenly had to kit out 'Mrs Shand Kydd's wee lassie', as he calls her, with the headgear appropriate to her new status. But when it came to her wedding dress, Lady Diana had her own ideas.

In November 1980 she was the subject of a personality sitting for *Vogue*. These are somewhat mysterious affairs, sometimes involving members of the royal family, like Princess Anne, or interesting society figures, as Lady Diana was deemed in those days to be. The well-spoken young ladies of *Vogue* scour the fashion houses to gather up the latest creations, and so it came to pass that a pale pink silk chiffon blouse with ruffled neck was hanging on the rail as Lady Diana was pondering what she would like to wear for her portrait by Lord Snowdon.

The blouse was the work of a young husband-and-wife team, David and Elizabeth Emanuel. Lady Diana chose their offering for the photo session, liked it and asked for their phone number. So a few days later Elizabeth Emanuel received a phone call and misheard the name as she wrote it down in the appointment book (no one just 'drops in' on the Emanuels: 'By appointment only' says their polished brass entry phone just across Brook Street from Claridges).

'She looks familiar,' thought Mrs Emanuel when the lady arrived.

In the course of the next few months Lady Diana bought several of the Emanuels' ensembles and, after the engagement was announced, she came to them for a smart ball gown for her first full-scale evening appearance. She had already scoured Beauchamp Place with no result, and was delighted to see, hanging on a rail, the shell of a low-cut black strapless creation which, the Emanuels told her, could be made up in days.

The result was That Dress. Until she appeared in it people had been almost patronizing about her maidenliness.

'Nineteen and no "past"? What has the girl been doing?'

The national dismay which greeted the generous display of its Queen-to-be's assets suggested that it was Britain which was old-fashioned.

One of the distinctions that she took some time to learn was the divide in her new life between public and private wear. For several months after the engagement she was still seen at polo matches in jeans and dungarees. She had had little call in her previous existence for formal daytime dresses: well-cut country suits and a handful of smart evening outfits were the only 'dressing up' clothes she had, and her first attempts at formality were not totally successful.

On Saturday, 21 February 1981, she went shopping at Simpson's in Piccadilly. She knew she would have to wear something respectable when her engagement was announced the following week, and not finding what she wanted in Simpson's she went down to Harrods. There in the ready-to-wear she saw hanging a blue, scallop-necked outfit by Cojana, a middle-of-the-road, off-the-peg British fashion house. It was conventional enough in all conscience. But, anxious to play safe, she asked for the skirt to be lengthened – with matronly consequences.

Since those first faltering steps, *Vogue* has taken her in hand. Her sisters Lady Jane and Lady Sarah both worked for the magazine before they got married, and in the summer of 1981 *Vogue*'s beauty editor, Felicity Clark, and a senior fashion editor, Anna Harvey, organized a crash course in what *Vogue* likes to call 'the options'. Using simple rails like the one from which the Emanuels struck it so lucky, they have introduced her to *dernier cri* young designers like Bruce Oldfield and Jasper Conran, and the Princess works out which of these clothes harmonize with her own dress ideas – slim skirts, not full ones, and an emphasis on her waist rather than on her legs.

Vogue, who forage similarly for Princess Michael and for the Duchess of Kent, are very anxious to emphasize that the Princess is definitely Mistress of her own Wardrobe.

'I don't think that the fact she looks so good has much to do with us,' says Felicity Clark. 'We only present clothes to her, as though she were in a shop, and then she chooses what she likes.'

But Vogue House makes a very convenient shop – and a discreet one too. The Princess's car drives down through the traffic in Maddox Street, slips right just before Sidney Rose, the tobacconist, into Masons Arms Mews, and vanishes into the darkness of the underground car park beneath Vogue House.

'The idea has been to bring the best of British fashion under her eye and

Christmas coat. The Princess of Wales outside the chapel at Windsor on Christmas morning, December 1981

The Princess look. Pearl choker for gala evenings ...

to help her,' says Felicity Clark, an old friend of the Spencer girls, and a charming example of the upper-crust ladies who, with working-class photographers, set the ground rules of British fashion.

Princesses of Wales, of course, set fashion rules of their own. Princess Alexandra, the first Princess of Wales after the development of the mass-circulation newspaper, and thus the first to become recognizable to people who had not actually met her in the flesh, had a small scar on her neck which she liked to hide with a broad pearl choker. The result was that broad pearl chokers became compulsory evening wear in late-Victorian society, and the predilection which the latest Princess of Wales has for the same item of decoration has led jewellers across the land to start making copies of it. Other trends set by the Princess of Wales include sapphire and diamond engagement rings (mail order copies start at £9, including VAT), ruffle-necked blouses, and her low-heeled court shoes which, as Suzy Menkes, fashion editor of *The Times*, puts it, have made 'a positive fashion statement out of the tactful necessity of bringing her height down to her husband's level.'

She has a long way to go, and the rush with which she kitted herself out for her new role in the summer of 1981 sometimes suggested a little girl let loose in a sweetie shop. Arriving one day on the corner by the Emanuels' first-floor salon, she walked by mistake into the showroom of Roland Klein below, and managed to buy herself a new outfit in the course of finding her way upstairs.

Rushing excitedly into John Boyd's hatbox-sized boutique in the Brompton Arcade, she waved the belt from an outfit she had just ordered from Bellville Sassoon down the street.

'Can I have a hat to match this, please?'

John Boyd (who also makes hats for Mrs Thatcher) did not have the heart to tell the girl that he really needed to see rather more of the clothes if he was to design a hat to top them off with glory. So he smiled fondly, found out her own ideas – and phoned Bellville Sassoon after she had gone.

'Now then, what's this you've been selling to the Lady Diana?'

Mr Boyd would not have it any other way.

'She'll come in and say, "You must be so cross with me, how I wore that hat yesterday,"' he says. 'But I always tell her she is learning fast.'

The ultimate reward for the men and women who dress the Princess of Wales continuously for three years will be the royal warrant, 'By Appointment' – Gina Fratini, Piero de Monzi, Manolo Blahnik and Donald Campbell are among the suppliers in contention – and for them the dividends could be large. The big buyers from Japan and America are traditionally supercilious towards British designers: they change their orders, cancel them and pay late without compunction. But since the spring of 1981 they have been reformed characters when dealing with designers whose products have been photographed on the Princess, and their orders have been substantial. Women the world over are evidently anxious to be dressed in the clothes that were made by a hand that dressed up the Princess of Wales – and the prospect of Japanese ladies teetering through Tokyo in scaled-down princess-kit is cheering in the year that British Leyland's only new car was designed by Honda. She is the best thing for British fashion since Carnaby Street.

Just the same, it is strange how the normally garrulous stars of fashion clam up at any mention of their illustrious client. They whisper the fact that 'she is very fond of *red*' or that she fidgets in fittings, as though their indiscretion could land them in the Tower, and wild horses will not drag from them the secret of secrets – how much she pays.

Right up to and including her scallop-necked engagement suit, Lady Diana Spencer was putting her clothes on her mother's account at Harrods. But now her purchases there all go through the special office which preserves the confidentiality of royal shopping. So Harrods will not comment on the fact, say, that the Princess was to be seen last October, on her way back from London Airport, where she waved off her husband to Anwar Sadat's funeral, popping into the store to treat herself to a new pair of elegant black jodhpurs. Bellville Sassoon recorded her early visits in the appointments book as 'Miss Buckingham'.

They could give lessons in discretion to Jean Machine in the Kings Road. When this emporium realized who had just bought a pair of blue denims from them for £15.95 in the summer of 1981, they photostatted the cheque and exhibited it proudly in the window.

... and low-heeled shoes for daytime duties

ome for the new Princess of Wales in London is a three-floor set of apartments round a courtyard in Kensington Palace. Her neighbours are two sets of her husband's cousins – the Gloucesters, and Prince and Princess Michael of Kent – and his aunt Margaret.

The Prince of Wales had worked out the main lines of his London base before his engagement, but in the spring and summer of 1981 the design was added to: a nursery, children's playroom and nanny's quarters above the main double bedroom, and off one side of the bedroom a pretty new bathroom, all marble and mirrors. Prince Charles's bathroom, off the other side, is in rather different style, and features an impressive polished wood antique which looks like a chest of drawers, but is, in fact, a commode. He collects them.

The private rooms are in modern style (the Waleses' decorator, Dudley Poplak, who made his name beautifying ocean liners, has a tendency to cover everything in suede, but the budget did not run to this), while the rooms in which the couple will entertain are more traditional, with flock wallpaper, carefully planned around masterpieces from the royal collections. There is a floor of offices to accommodate the private secretaries, his aides and her ladies-in-waiting; two lifts, a large music room beside the breakfast room – very convenient for morning tap-dancing sessions – all manner of staff and domestic quarters, including a room devoted to the washing of crystal (the sink itself is made of wood as well as the draining board), and, on top of the roof, a ranch-fenced barbecue pit nestling between the William and Mary chimneys. Just north of the front door, beyond the garages, is a helicopter pad.

There is another such pad down at the Princess's country home, Highgrove, a square-looking Georgian mansion beside the A433 from Bath to Cirencester in Gloucestershire. The house is clearly visible from the road, and a footpath runs right along one low wall, to the delight of photographers with long-focus lenses. It evidently did not occur to Prince Charles, when he bought the house in the summer of 1980, that he was going to have a wife so adorable that he would want to kiss her on the front doorstep and dance with her on the lawn.

Highgrove, beside the A433

'No one could pretend,' write the authors of *Royal Homes in Gloucestershire*, with some regret, 'that Highgrove was ever in the top flight of country houses in the county.' It is certainly less stylish than Gatcombe Park, six miles away, where Princess Anne and Mark Phillips took up residence in 1976, and it is an ill-kept secret that the Phillipses considered Highgrove and rejected it when they were looking for a home in the area. In a bid to smarten Highgrove's image a little, the townsfolk of Tetbury made their wedding present to the Prince and Princess of Wales an imposing set of wrought-iron gates.

Dudley Poplak has been at work on the interior. He has decorated the hall a muted pink, using the currently fashionable technique of rag-rolling, which looks a little as if the Seven Dwarfs have been let loose with mops and paint pots. It certainly makes for a cheerful welcome. The main drawing room is green, with prettily fringed and draped curtains, and there are a lot of small tables set around. Most of the floors are polished natural wood. When a BBC camera crew went to Highgrove to interview the Prince of Wales at the end of 1981, the ambience made them all feel very much at home.

'How's the missus then?' inquired the sparks, who, in the tradition of BBC camera crews, regarded himself as at least the equal of the subject he was filming.

'Ah, quite well, thank you,' replied the Prince of Wales. 'She's finding pregnancy harder work than she expected.'

The interview ended around lunchtime.

'Would you like something to eat?' inquired the Prince, and led the way into the kitchen where he rummaged in the pantry. He emerged proudly bearing slices of quiche and the raw material for ham sandwiches, which he proceeded to prepare for the benefit of his guests.

'Thirsty?' he inquired, and vanished down into the cellar, reappearing shortly afterwards a little redfaced at the strain of heaving a crate of beer up into the drawing room. It was a special consignment of wedding ale, bearing his own portrait and that of the new Princess.

'A present from the brewery,' he said apologetically. 'I don't know what it tastes like, but you're very welcome to try it.'

Highgrove was turned out by an unknown architect between 1796 and 1798 for the Paul family, a clan of pious Huguenot immigrants with names like Onesiphorus and Obadiah. Memorials to the Paul family in Tetbury church, whose sharp spire is visible from the house, show a couple of naval heroes, but attempts to link them genealogically to the House of Windsor earn more marks for enterprise than for credibility: 'the latter's first wife was the grand-daughter of the eighth Earl of Strathmore, from whom the Queen Mother is descended.'

Gloucestershire, in fact, does not boast a notably royal history. King Edward II came to a gruesome end in Berkeley Castle, and one Prince of Wales was actually killed at Tewkesbury. The stubborn resistance which the county town of Gloucester put up to Charles I was a significant factor in his loss of the civil war – and the siege which photographers put down around the Princess of Wales when she moved into Highgrove in the autumn of 1981 displayed distinct *lèse majesté*.

Coming out of a local sweetshop one day that November the Princess was ambushed by a marauding photographer, and next day the *Daily Mail* listed her purchases – Roses chocolates, some fudge, a packet of Revels, and some strawberry Chewits.

Consulted subsequently, the sweetshop owner, Mr Richard Stigwood, indignantly denied that any of these brands were now entitled to the royal warrant.

'I'm not going to tell the newspapers what the Princess buys if she calls at my shop,' he protested.

Mr Stigwood spoke for all of Tetbury. The townsfolk were delighted with their new lady of the manor, and they were not going to let curious outsiders frighten her away. Ask a Tetbury shopkeeper when the Princess last honoured him with her custom and if he does not recognize you, his reply will be noncommittal. If you are wearing a trenchcoat or carrying a camera with a long lens, he is likely to be downright surly.

Not that the shopkeepers can complain too loudly, since they must be one of the few communities of British retailers for whom 1981 showed an upswing in business. Tetbury is now thronged with cars at weekends, and coach parties are expected in the summer.

'She's put five thousand pounds on the value of most property round here,' says Jim Gilmore, whose card reads 'Equestrian and Agricultural Journalists, Public Relations Commissions'. 'The sort of house that cost fifty-five thousand one year ago is priced now nearer sixty.'

Gilmore has been covering local stories since the end of the Second

Click! Even sweetshopping was news. The Princess snapped in Tetbury

World War, and he has not done badly himself from the world's sudden interest in Tetbury's first resident princess. But he cherishes her as fiercely as his neighbours do.

'I remember the first time I saw her in the street, before she got married, when she was just down there to visit the place. I thought, "Who the devil's that?" Then I realized. "It's Lady Di!" There was nobody with her, no detective even, and I knew at once I'd got a story. But I thought, "Let her go." Why should I tell all of Fleet Street?'

Jim Gilmore is proud he did not take his thirty pieces of silver, but reality could not be kept at bay for ever. Once the royal peal of bells had rung out from Tetbury church on the weekend the couple moved in, the lure of the Princess's bubblegum expeditions proved too strong. The White Hart beside Tetbury's pillared town hall joined El Vino's and Harry's Bar on the circuit of international watering holes where photographers rest their shutter-fingers. Whenever the Princess was at Highgrove in the autumn of 1981, the White Hart was packed, and waitresses bore sizzling trays of toasted sandwiches into the downstairs lounge for the anorak-clad sleuths as they returned from their labours in the chilly Cotswold countryside.

Mine host of the White Hart would sigh when asked how many bedrooms his hotel could offer. 'Just twelve,' he would say. 'I could have filled fifty at times since the Princess came.'

Until 8 December 1981, that is. Then Queen Elizabeth II summoned Fleet Street's editors to her, and by that evening most of George Wortley's guests had packed up their camera bags and aimed their cars towards the M4 – for the time being at least.

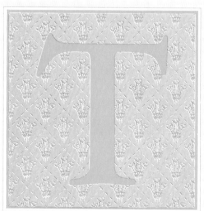

The Queen's decision to do something about the press was triggered by the news that her daughter-in-law was expecting a baby, and the public announcement of the Princess's pregnancy on 5 November 1981 played a major part in producing the reverence with which the royal plea was heard.

This bore out Professor Leach's theory on the symbolism of royal procreation, since it was not strictly necessary for the Prince and Princess of Wales to have children: the succession to the British throne is more than assured by several football teams of designated heirs, starting with the Princes Andrew and Edward. But Britain and the world would have felt something was amiss if Charles and Diana had not, of their own flesh and blood, created life to succeed them. So the Princess did her duty – and in record time. In 1948 the future Queen Elizabeth II produced her baby six days before her first wedding anniversary; in 1982 HRH the Princess of Wales was scheduled to improve on this by a month.

The new mother-to-be gave every sign of finding her procreative responsibilities exactly what she wanted for herself. She could not wait to dress up in maternity clothes, and she took to wearing a tent coat long before it was strictly necessary. As was her way, the subject on her mind became the subject of her conversations at public engagements, and this led to a certain grumbling among ladies who had no choice but to work every day until the seventh month of pregnancy, morning sickness or not.

The royal event provided, as usual, the opportunity to elevate a routine domestic phenomenon into a national talking point. Agony aunties published carefree pregnancy tips, fashion editors featured maternity wear, and Britain went broody for a season – if not to everyone's delight. 'Sir,' wrote Mr Peter Wilson of Pudsey, West Yorkshire, to the *Guardian* on 12 November 1981: 'You report the Lord Mayor of London as saying about the royal pregnancy: "Babies are bits of star-dust blown from the hand of God." Gets right up your nose as well, does stardust.'

In the *Sunday Times* Veronica Horwell lamented the end of the summer fairy tale. Romance had changed too quickly to dynastic history for her taste, and she made some sharp points about the example this set to other young women, encouraging them to rush into motherhood before they had fully enjoyed and explored themselves as individuals or as marriage partners.

Other young women did not seem to agree with Ms Horwell. Polled by Capital Radio, young married women getting off buses in the City of London said that they would just love to stop work and have lots of babies if only they could afford it, and had a couple of nursery maids to help.

But the larger point remained. Lady Di had vanished too soon. She had been an individual for a few months, an idiosyncratic, enticing personality in her own right. With her marriage she had become one of a pair, and now she was about to submerge herself in a family of three, four – who could tell how many, since she had once expressed the ambition to have more children than Queen Victoria?

While sharing in her obvious happiness, some people felt a little cheated. The dragonfly had emerged from the chrysalis to shimmer for only a summer. Coleherne Court, the wicked Whitaker, the wedding-dress capers, the honeymoon, all this had quickened the national pulse. Was the glamorous Princess lost for ever? As late as February 1982 the *Sun* and the *Daily Star* felt their readers required photographic reassurance that the mother-to-be, sunning her tummy in the supposed seclusion of a Bahamas beach, could still provide a right royal pin-up. Few of their readers had ever doubted it.

he is one of those sweet creatures who seem to come from the skies to help and bless poor mortals.' Queen Victoria's praise of her new daughter-in-law, Princess Alexandra, finds its echoes 120 years later: 'a simple, natural girl, with the large and tender heart of a woman who has had a far wider experience of life ... now compelled to take the foremost position in the society of the greatest and richest capital in the world.... Her dignity of manner in society has struck everyone.'

Once upon a time a princess reposed at the summit of a hierarchy – countesses, marchionesses, duchesses, they formed a social pyramid which lent support to the royal capstone. Today a princess must float in more lonely eminence, loved and admired by an egalitarian world, but ultimately dependent upon its whim.

'Monarchy is only as good as the people doing the job,' the late Lord Mountbatten liked to say. 'It is safe in the hands of people like the Queen and Prince Charles because they have characters which the world loves and admires.' He would then go on to specify certain living members of the royal family whose characters did not, in his opinion, inspire love and respect, and in whose hands, therefore, the monarchy would not be safe.

Were Lord Louis alive today, there can be no doubt in which category he would place Diana, HRH the Princess of Wales and future British Queen. Her weaknesses are her strengths. People love her for her anxieties and vulnerabilities, her tendency to speak before she thinks – her scattiness even.

'Oh, Ma'am, haven't you got a big head?' said the fitter at Locks, the exclusive hatters, courtesy being temporarily overwhelmed by surprise at the measurement just taken.

'Don't worry,' replied the Princess. 'There's really very little inside.' In Hollywood Miss Goldie Hawn has based an entire career on less.

At the Speaker's Dinner in the House of Commons in December 1981, the Princess of Wales found herself sitting beside David Steel, the leader of the Liberal Party.

'They must have sat me beside you,' she said to him, 'because I'm so young.'

The Liberal leader took this as a compliment to his own youthfulness, rather than to any incipient grandfatherliness, and he spent the meal in animated conversation with his charming young companion. After the loyal toast he reached for a cigar and started to break off the band with obvious anticipation of the pleasure ahead, when suddenly he remembered that the lady was pregnant.

'Oh dear, I am so sorry,' he said with embarrassment, putting the cigar down again.

'Don't worry at all,' said the Princess, who hates tobacco smoke even at the best of times. Then she picked up the cigar, placed one end firmly in Mr Steel's mouth, and applied a lighted match to the other.

Now perhaps princesses are not supposed to behave in this fashion, but this one does.

'What a long time to sit!' she exclaimed after her first official engagement. 'I've got pins and needles in my bottom.'

Informed by one little boy in Wales that his daddy had instructed him to give the Princess a kiss, she did not hesitate. 'You'd better give me one, then,' she said, and bent down to proffer him her cheek.

'Like a piece of unseasoned natural wood,' wrote *Woman's Own* in April 1981, 'she is ready to be fashioned into a stately and polished figurehead.' Let us hope that they are wrong. It is her lack of pomposity which is so refreshing, the fact that she clearly has to steel herself for many of her new public tasks, and that beneath her recent dignity she is still, in essence, just a kid. Sometimes, trying to disguise her height, she stoops somewhat, pushing her knees together, and then her long legs splay out from each other almost like a foal's. Experienced members of the royal family have developed a sleight of hand for disposing of the little presents which it has become the custom for crowds to hand over during walkabouts, but she has not yet mastered this technique. One afternoon in Wales her eyes suddenly flashed with that famous look of panic as she realized that her arms were overflowing with the bouquets she had been collecting – so, spinning round on one low heel, she just dumped them all into the arms of a lady-in-waiting.

Christmas carols. The Princess visits Guildford Cathedral, December 1981

The little girl whom her family called 'Duchess' will become regal soon enough. Prince Charles likes to repeat the advice given him in his courting days by one old estate worker at Sandringham – 'Take a good look at their mothers, master, afore yer makes up yer mind' – and, being a cautious character, the Prince has presumably taken this counsel to heart. At the royal wedding several observers remarked that the one non-royal lady who looked as though she could be royal was Mrs Shand Kydd.

The Princess can be tough enough when the occasion calls for it. The fact that she blushes a lot does not mean that she lacks the ability to get exactly what she wants. In love with Prince Charles, she succeeded where girls who were much older and more liberated – and who had many more O-Levels – all failed, and she has also managed to create a private relationship with one of the world's most public men.

The effect on him has been dramatic. Lost in his bachelorhood, and rather closer to forty in character than in years, Prince Charles chose to surround himself with men whose age and tastes showed him up to advantage. By comparison with his friend Nicholas Soames, he was lithe, well-thatched and socially adventurous, mingling with all levels of society, professionally at least. Compared to his private secretary, Edward Adeane, whose father and great-grandfather were courtiers before him, the Prince was unstuffy, unconventional even. But set alongside other young British males in their early thirties, his style was really quite sedate – and behind the public image of the devil-may-care Lothario was a solitary and sometimes almost forlorn character, who confided in his valet and who spent a surprising number of evenings having dinner on his own at home.

Now add ingredient X. Today Prince Charles is transparently a happy man, at ease with himself. In the autumn of 1981 he and his new wife were to be seen walking the corridors of Buckingham Palace hand in hand. In private, friends report that they cling to each other adoringly, and in public they are sometimes notably difficult to prise apart – aides almost have to bully them to navigate separate paths through receptions. Free to choose, they would clearly much prefer to be left in a corner to exchange their own gentle gossip and private endearments.

'Bother,' says Prince Charles, shifting his toe to look at something that his shoe has picked up from his sitting-room carpet, 'another of my wife's sweets' – and he looks so happy about it.

She has spread this happiness widely. In less than a year this girl has become part of every British family, the relative everyone knows, loves and gossips about fondly, even if she never actually comes to call – an emblem and mascot that is fiercely cherished. Favoured customers of Bellville Sassoon treasure little cantaloup silk snippings off the bolt from which her going-away outfit was cut. Her portrait hangs in the National Portrait Gallery behind the same bulletproof perspex that protects the Mona Lisa.

Cynics would liken the Princess's meteoric ascent into the stratosphere of the national imagination to the other great success story of 1981, the rise of the Social Democratic Party, whose success stems from people's dissatisfaction with everything else in Britain and upon the party's extraordinary ability to avoid specifying exactly what it would do to put things right. But royalty is not politics. That is the point of having a constitutional monarchy and of lavishing upon it the affection, loyalty and respect which are far too precious to be bestowed upon politicians.

'A nation can fail to get the money supply right and yet survive,' said the Archbishop of Canterbury in July 1981, trying to explain why the royal wedding mattered. 'But no nation that fails to respond to the ideal of self-giving and generous love will survive as a united or a healthy community. These are the truths on which we should build our family life and human relations, and they are the truths which we look to the royal family to exemplify.'

Foreign commentators worried greatly at the time of the royal wedding at the way in which the society which created Toxteth and Brixton could indulge in such a binge. Was it escapism? Was it schizophrenia?

It was neither. The ruins of Toxteth were tokens of imperfection – injustice, envy, anger, the things that are wrong with the human condition. The royal wedding provided a focus around which people could set other feelings – hope, gentleness, understanding, those qualities of civilized humanity and family life which the House of Windsor works so hard to represent.

The point about myths, says Professor Sir Edmund Leach, is not that they are false. On the contrary, for believers they are profoundly true. But the fantasy they enshrine is usually the inverse of life's cold reality: we credit God with immortality because experience tells us that we are all mortal, while the virtues which we credit to members of the royal family are those which we would like for ourselves, but which we know we can never attain in full perfection.

'Lady Di' has now joined that family to whose basic human transactions the world chooses to accord such significance. The British monarchy has been described as 'a fragile mystery that works', and the Princess of Wales has brought a new twist to its old magic. Young, beautiful, married to a prince and now enjoying all the comforts and privileges which accompany the very unrepresentative life style of representative royalty, she could easily become the object of envy in an unhealthily envious society. Instead she generates love, admiration and a very warm glow.

This is principally because of the special status she has acquired through her marriage. Today we call her 'Your Royal Highness'; in the fullness of time she should become 'Your Majesty'. But this book has tried to show how she has also brought something of her own to the lifetime's work on which she has embarked. There is her sense of style, there is her humour, and there is the ease with which she can communicate the vivacity and naturalness of her feelings. Queen Elizabeth II is not, frankly, always very good at this. She finds it difficult to get across the warmth and humour that she shares with friends. In public she can be rather stiff with children. But her new daughter-in-law is a natural.

This naturalness is a quality that the new Princess shares with her grandmother-in-law, Queen Elizabeth the Queen Mother, and this may have something to do with the fact that neither of them grew up in palaces. Well born though they were, both women started out their lives as one of us, not one of them, and perhaps it is twenty years spent reading the papers, rather than being in them, that leads to gestures like taking round slices of your wedding cake to the ladies who sew up your clothes.

It also makes for a literally enchanting transformation when you are the one plucked out of millions to dance at the ball. The glass slipper was missing, but the youngest sister from a broken home did get the gown, the glass coach and, of course, the charming prince. The wand was waved by us because we want her to carry and keep alive our hopes and dreams and fantasies.

It is important to us that the magic does not die – and that is why we have a special reason for hoping that Diana, Her Royal Highness the Princess of Wales, may truly live happily ever after.

Princess in blue jeans. Shopping in Balmoral, August 1981

Author's acknowledgements

After the publication of *Majesty* I was frequently asked what advice I would give to anyone writing a book about the British royal family. I invariably replied that the last place an aspiring author should think of going was to the Press Office of Buckingham Palace, and I am happy for the opportunity publicly to retract that now without reservation. The help I have received in the preparation of this book from Buckingham Palace, and from the Queen's Press Secretary, Michael Shea, in particular, has been generous and frank – though the responsibility for any errors is my own.

The Princess of Wales has generated a formidable corpus of literature in the course of her twelve months in the public eye, and I have drawn heavily on this, so I gratefully acknowledge the information I have taken from articles by Alison Miller and by Ian Jack in the *Sunday Times*, by Tom Davies in the *Observer*, by Edward Steen in the *Sunday Telegraph*, by Suzy Menkes and by Hugh Noyes in *The Times*, by Alan Rusbridger in the *Guardian*, and by Tina Brown in *Tatler*.

Settling Down by James Whitaker (Quartet, 1981), *Royal Wedding* by Gordon Honeycombe (Michael Joseph, 1981), and *Royal Homes in Gloucestershire* by Geoffrey Sanders and David Verey (Alan Sutton, 1981) have also been consulted.

A number of people generously gave me information off the record, and in addition I would like to thank for their help: Nicholas and Anne Colquhoun-Denvers; Des Carwardine; David and Elizabeth Emanuel; Alastair Forbes; David Frost; James Gilmore; Annabel Harper; Nicholas Haslam; Anthony Holden; Angela de Klee; Gregorio Kohon; Professor Sir Edmund Leach; Suzy Menkes; David Nicholas; Michael Roberts; David Roy; Audrey Russell; Jennifer Sharp; Godfrey Smith; Edda Tasiemka and the Hans Tasiemka archive; James Whitaker; and the librarians of Chatham House and of the London Library.

This is the shortest book I have ever written. It has also been the most enjoyable, not least because it is the product of an efficient and cheerful team. So I would like to record my special thanks to John Cushman and to Michael Shaw for their unfailing encouragement, to Jacqueline Williams for her diligent research work in some most arcane areas, to Frances Ullman for her advice and indefatigable typing in the production of the manuscript, to my parents for their proof-reading, to my wife Sandi for her criticism of the text and for her support of me –and, not least, to my children, Sasha and Scarlett, who did not see as much of me over Christmas 1981 as they should have done.

Robert Lacey
January 1982